Don't Talk to the Wall!

Understanding Personality Types

David Gibson

Cluain Mhuire Press
2014

Tables and Diagrams

No part of this book may be reproduced in any form or by any electronic or mechanical means, including information storage and retrieval systems, without permission in writing from the publisher, except by a reviewer, who may quote brief passages in a review. Any members of educational institutions wishing to photocopy part or all of the work for classroom use, or publishers who would like to obtain permission in include the work in an anthology, should send their inquiries to: Cluain Mhuire Press (Copyright), 42 Glasnevin Avenue, Dublin 11, Ireland.

Published by Cluain Mhuire Press and Createspace

Set in 12 point Cambria

Copyright © 2014 David Gibson
All rights reserved.

ISBN-10: 1499745397
ISBN-13: 978-1499745399

DEDICATION

To friends who have shaped my life.

Table of Contents

CONTENTS

1. The Beginning of Our Journey — 1
2. Setting Out — 9
3. The Essential Ingredients — 22
4. Conditional Love — 30
5. The Creative Daydreamer — 43
6. The Brilliant Sceptic — 53
7. The Charming Manipulator — 64
8. The Responsible Workaholic — 75
9. The Enthusiastic Over-Reactor — 86
10. The Playful Resister — 96
11. A View of Time — 105
12. A Bird's Eye View — 113
13. It Takes All Sorts — 121
14. Channels of Communication — 132
15. Instead of Talking to the Wall — 139
16. Permissions — 148
17. Transformation — 155

References — 169
Suggested Further Reading — 172
Author Index — 173
Subject Index — 174

TABLES AND DIAGRAMS

Figures:

1.	The Doors Of Communication	16
2.	Open Target and Trapdoors	18
3.	The Ego State Model	24
4.	Contaminations	25
5.	The Functional Model of Ego States	28
6.	The Withdrawal of the Creative Daydreamer	49
7.	Exclusion of the Child Ego State	60
8.	Exclusion of the Parent Ego State	71
9.	Contamination by the Parent Ego State	82
10.	Contamination by the Child Ego State	91
11.	The Parent-Child Impasse	101
12.	A Bird's Eye View	113
13.	The Cycle of Inquiry	146
14.	The Enneagram	158

Tables:

1.	Personality Adaptations	13
2.	Drivers, Process Scripts & Types	106
3.	Behaviour Doors of Personality Adaptations	116
4.	Feeling Doors of Personality Adaptations	117
5.	Thinking Doors of Personality Adaptations	118

ACKNOWLEDGMENTS

I want to acknowledge the illustrations that Br Joe Connolly kindly agreed to draw. They capture some aspects of the various personality types with a gentle and wry humour. Thanks Joe!

Thanks especially to Dr Cathy McQuaid who took the time and trouble to check the book for accuracy. Her comments and ideas were a great help in clarifying the key concepts of personality adaptations. She was also ever vigilant with regard to grammatical errors! Thank you Cathy. If there are any mistakes or inaccuracies in the text, I take full responsibility for them.

A special thanks to the Vicentini Family – Stefano, Lori, Sara, Maria Chiara and Isacco - who offered me generous hospitality in their beautiful house in the Val di Rabbi while I was still working on this book.

Thanks are also due to Tim Leyland who challenged me to make the concepts in the book crystal clear. If I haven't succeeded in this, it's not Tim's fault. He was robust in his request for clarity and accuracy.

And finally, I want to thank Vann Joines for reading through the draft document and offering some valuable comments.

CHAPTER ONE

The Beginning of Our Journey

*"We don't receive wisdom;
we must discover it for ourselves after a journey
that no one can take for us or spare us."*
Marcel Proust

In the play *Shirley Valentine* by Willy Russell (1986), Shirley begins to talk to the wall in her kitchen. As she prepares her husband's egg and chips, she chats with her wall:

> -Hiya Wall! What's wrong with that? There's a woman three doors down talks to her microwave. Talking to a microwave! Wall, what's the world coming to?

Shirley had come to the stage when it was easier to talk to her kitchen wall than to communicate with her husband. She might as well have been talking to the wall as trying to have a meaningful conversation with her partner. She had reached the stage where communication had broken down, and the wall seemed more receptive to her thoughts and feelings. At least it didn't argue or answer back!

How often do we find that the person we want to communicate with simply doesn't listen, or seems to pick up what we are saying, and then twists it into something we never intended to mean. Communication can be complicated and frustrating. As a result, we often withdraw when we discover that the other person doesn't get what we mean, or we find ourselves in the middle of an argument that blows up out of the blue.

George Bernard Shaw, wisely said, 'The single biggest problem in communication is the illusion that it has taken place' (quoted in Caroselli, 2000:71). We may think we are getting through to someone, only to find that they literally have turned a deaf ear. What is it that makes communication so difficult? Why do we seem to disconnect with those we love, when all we are trying to do is share our thoughts and feelings, and let the other person know what we are thinking and feeling in the moment?

Don't Talk to the Wall

In *Don't Talk to the Wall!* I will explore why we can find ourselves wanting to talk to the wall rather than have deep and meaningful conversations with those we love. When we are driven up the wall in the face of miss-communication, *Don't Talk to the Wall!* will, I hope, show how we can do something about breakdowns in communication. Once we understand what is going on between ourselves and the other person who seems to react negatively to us, we can begin to change our approach to them. Changing our approach involves changing our language.

The Language of Communication

When we find that we are speaking a different language with someone, we can be sending messages to other people until we are blue in the face, but the other person simply doesn't understand the language we are using. We are metaphorically whistling in the dark. Hence, we need to learn *their* language before we can have any hope of reaching them. We need to get on their wavelength so that our signals can be picked up and understood by the other person.

The languages I am talking about are the three languages of thinking, feeling and behaviour. If the person I am talking to is a thinking person, then I need to use thinking language with them in order that we can communicate clearly. If, on the other hand, the person is a feeling person, then I need to use feeling language for both of us to communicate well. For other people who understand the language of behaviour, then I need to use that same language to get in contact with them.

In *Don't Talk to the Wall!* I will introduce you to a fascinating model of communication that will go far to make talking to the wall unnecessary and ultimately unsatisfying. I also offer the technique of listening that forms the basis for good communication.

More importantly, *Don't Talk to the Wall!* introduces a model of personality types that will help explain why communication with people often fails when we do not understand the differences that exist in personalities.

Models of Personality Types

Many people may already have some knowledge of other models of personality typologies. The Myers-Briggs Type Indicator Test offers a useful insight into how people see and interact with the world (Myers-Briggs, 1980). The Enneagram also provides an invaluable key to understanding our basic compulsions, and how we can work to redeem these basic flaws (Riso & Hudson, 1999). Both these models have proved valuable both in the business world, and also in the lives of ordinary people. So, why is there need for another model?

Don't Talk to the Wall! offers a different approach to communication that focuses on the way we have learnt from an early age to adapt our personality to people, and how these *personality adaptations* impact on the way we manage our lives, and how we interact with others. We will see how personality adaptations require specific ways of managing interpersonal communication in order for relationships to grow and develop.

Personality Types or Adaptations?

Throughout the book I will use the phrase personality adaptation or personality type interchangeably. Whereas initially I will refer to them more as adaptation, later I will stress them as personality types as this description places them in the same context as other personality types. In a sense, the adaptation refers to the mechanism within the person to develop a particular personality type in response to the demands of parents or caregivers. People adapt to the way they were brought up, and develop a personality type that best suits the situation in which they found themselves. People adapt and then form personality types that describe their way of thinking, feeling and behaving.

Personality Adaptations

What do I mean by personality adaptations? The phrase comes from a psychiatrist called Dr Paul Ware who did some great work with 'difficult' adolescents in residential care (Ware, 1983). Over the course of his work with them, he came to realize that he could classify their behaviours along a number of clear patterns and in response to the way they were treated from early childhood. By recognizing these patterns, he understood that each adaptation needed to be responded to in a particular manner in order to make effective connections with the young people.

Paul later worked with Taibi Kahler who developed an approach called The Process Communication Model, which further enriched this model and offered valuable insights into this theory (Kahler, 1978; 1979; 2008). However, in *Don't Talk to the Wall*, we will not be going into such depth, but will be using their ideas to help us understand how we can better communicate with those we love, and with those we sometimes find difficult to connect with.

I should not omit to acknowledge the work of Vann Joines and Ian Stewart who wrote a fabulous book on personality adaptations and on which much of this book is based (Joines & Stewart, 2002). For anyone who wants to go into a deeper study of personality adaptations I can strongly recommend the work of Ian and Vann. They really took all the elements of personality adaptations and brought them together into an elegant model. So, why, you may ask, is there need for this book if there is already a fine book that explains the model perfectly?

Why Another Book on Communication?

My hope is that *Don't Talk to the Wall!* Will bring the theory into the lives of people who do not intend to become therapists or psychologists, but who want to understand themselves and others so as to communicate better. We all want to connect with those we love, and I firmly believe that a good understanding of personality adaptations will go a long way to help us do this. So, I want to make this theory accessible to everyone, and to share my own excitement that I felt when I first came across this approach to various personality types.

I believe that understanding the different personality types or adaptations will greatly benefit people who struggle at times to understand where others are coming from.

By way of explanation, I should introduce myself as a practicing psychotherapist who trained in Transactional Analysis, and who discovered the power of this approach to therapy both personally and within my experience of working in organisations. It was during this time of training that I came across personality adaptations, which fits well with Transactional Analysis.

Transactional Analysis and Personality Types

I want to place both the personality types and listening skills in the context of Transactional Analysis (TA), a fascinating theory developed in the early 1960s by Eric Berne.

In Chapter 2, I outline the broad strokes of the theory of personality that Paul Ware and Taibi Kahler devised, which I will then flesh out when I come to describe each of the different personality types.

In Chapter 3, I outline a brief summary of a few of the core elements of TA as this will make for a richer understanding of this classification of personalities.

Then, in Chapter 4, I explain the driving forces that go to create the various personality types that characterise this particular model.

These initial chapters (Chapters 2, 3 & 4) outline the main ideas that form the basis for personality types. Although somewhat theoretical, it is worth taking the time and effort to read these chapters carefully in order to understand the basis for the theory of personality types. By so doing, the description of the various adaptations will fit into the jigsaw neatly and clearly, and ensure that the overall theory is fully grasped.

Don't Skip Ahead!

You may be tempted to skip the next three chapters and get to the personality adaptations themselves. Resist the temptation because many of the terms used in the descriptions of the personality types or adaptations are explained in these initial chapters. If you do skip them, you may miss out somewhat on the theory behind the personality types, and find yourself always coming back to these chapters that explain the dynamics that underpin this typology. So, I suggest you enjoy the journey of discovery and begin at the beginning. As you set out, I hope you gather enough of the theory to gain a clear picture of each of the personality types or adaptations.

At the end of each short chapter on the individual personality adaptations (Chapters 5 to 10), I have listed a number of statements or beliefs that a particular personality adaptation might have. As you read through these beliefs you may get a better idea as to which of the personality adaptations you find characterise your approach to life. So, I suggest you mark the number of these beliefs that are true for you, and then when you have finished reading all the personality types, you will have a better idea of which type best suits you. It is good to remember that no self-selecting questionnaire is fool proof but they provide an indication as to the likely personality type you are.

Personality Adaptation Questionnaire

For a more objective assessment of your personality adaptations or types, you may wish to complete the Joines Personality Adaptation Questionnaire (JPAQ) devised by Vann Joines which can be found at the following website: http://www.seinstitute.com/jpaq/index.php?option=com_content&view=article&id=150&Itemid=58, and which can be filled in there at a modest cost. But again, I offer a suggestion that you wait until you have finished reading *Don't Talk to the Wall! before* you take the test by Joines. Having read the book, you will have a better idea of the implications of your particular adaptations.

CHAPTER TWO

Setting Out

> "Are you lost, Daddy?" I asked tenderly.
> "Shut up," he explained.
> Ring Lardner

When a child is born it is dependent on the mother or caregiver for its existence. It is helpless, and without the care and love of the mother or caring other, the child will not survive. The study of neuroscience now shows that even the brain of the baby will not develop properly unless it experiences the loving gaze of the mother. We now know that the cortex of a child is only in its rudimentary stage of development and needs the mother's right brain to draw out the right brain of the child (Schore, 2003; 2012). When love is absent or not in sufficient supply, the child will be negatively affected in its capacity to relate emotionally with others, and consequently will find it almost impossible to regulate affect.

The child then in the first few years of life is totally dependent on the mother's willingness to offer love and nourishment. When the love and acceptance of parents is not unconditional, the children have to adapt.

Children Have to Adapt

As children grow, develop and begin to speak, they instinctively come to realise that if they are to survive, they need to adapt to the demands of the mother or

Setting Out

caregivers. As a baby, all they had to do was cry, and the mother would see to their needs. But, gradually it dawns on the child that they are not that omnipotent, and that they often will have to adapt to the will of the parent and, at times, forego their needs to suit the availability of their parents. This is the beginning of the formation of personality adaptations.

The Six Personality Types or Adaptations

There are six personality types that children can learn and adopt. Indeed we all have some of these six adaptations to a greater of lesser degree. These are learned behaviours, which then become our automatic responses to people with whom we come in contact.

Each of these adaptations has a positive and a not so positive side to them, and it is this dual aspect of the adaptations that offers an exciting and fascinating key to understanding ourselves and others. The six adaptations are: Creative-Daydreamer, Brilliant-Sceptic, Charming-Manipulator, Responsible-Workaholic, Enthusiastic Over-Reactor and Playful-Resister (Joines, 1986:152-160; Kahler, 1979).

Six Personality Types

1. **Creative Daydreamer**
2. **Brilliant Sceptic**
3. **Charming Manipulator**
4. **Responsible Workaholic**
5. **Enthusiastic Over-Reactor**
6. **Playful Resister**

So, were we to see someone as a daydreamer who is always sceptical and manipulating, and who becomes a workaholic, over reacting to others while continually resisting any form of control – we do not have a positive picture of the person. But that picture only refers to the second element in each of the personality adaptations – the negative side so to speak.

On the other hand, imagine someone who is creative, brilliant, charming and responsible, while being enthusiastic and playful! Obviously, this presents an extremely positive portrait of a mature and integrating adult. But again, this only looks at the good side of our personality without the counterbalance of the shadow side.

We have all the Qualities of the Personality Types!

The reality of personality adaptations is that we have a combination of these twelve qualities, and that each of the dual qualities develops alongside the other. So, the Charming Manipulator may be charming, but they will also be somewhat manipulative. A Responsible Workaholic may be responsible, but they will have a tendency to overwork. This goes for each of the personality types. In a sense, we can view them as a scale where we inhabit a specific space along the continuum between the two elements of any personality adaptation. So, for instance, I may be more towards brilliance and further away from scepticism in the Brilliant Sceptic or vice versa, and the same being true of each of the six adaptations. We could say that each of the personality types has a shadow side to them, and the combination makes for a particular approach we have to people, and a

Setting Out

specific response we also may have to these same people.

The six adaptations can be subdivided into two sets of three adaptations: surviving and performing adaptations (Ware, 1983).

Surviving Personality Types

It is generally held that the surviving adaptations develop during the first few, preverbal years of life when the child is struggling to survive. This is the stage of real dependence on the part of children for their basic needs of care, nourishment and stimulation. Without these basic necessities children will shrivel up and die (Spitz, 1945). The surviving adaptations are: Creative-Daydreamer, Brilliant-Sceptic, and Charming Manipulator.

In order, therefore, for children to grow and develop, they have to be creative, brilliant and charming to attract the mother to respond to its basic needs, and it may also need to withdraw, manipulate and be vigilant when these needs are not forthcoming. So, the combinations of the surviving adaptations ensure the survival of the child. Needless to say, all of these processes are unconscious, and neither the mother nor child is fully aware of the dynamic going on. The mother-child interaction happens instinctively and both parties engage in this dance of life with the mother more or less unaware of what is happening in the interaction, and the child totally unaware.

Performing Personality Types

As the child grows and develops, it begins also to recognise that if it is to be loved and accepted, it needs to behave in ways that meet the parents' approval. This is when the performing adaptations kick in. In order for the child to be loved, the child soon realises that it needs to be responsible, enthusiastic or playful. The child also finds that the conditional nature of the parents' acceptance causes certain tensions in the child. For some, they feel a compulsion to be overly conscientious. For others, they become somewhat histrionic and over-reactive, while yet others dig in their heels and resist any attempt on the part of parents to control them. So, the performing adaptations of the Responsible-Workaholic, the Enthusiastic Over-Reactor and the Playful Resister all develop in response to the demands of parents, caregivers and the very cultural environment which influence the child to be and act in certain ways as a condition for their approval.

While it is important to stress that these performing adaptations are to some extent out of awareness, there is some level of consciousness in the process of adaptation as children begin to see the need to adapt to their parents and others in order to gain acceptance.

In Table 1 below I have listed the personality types or adaptation with the surviving adaptations below the heavy line, indicating the rather subconscious nature of

Responsible -Workaholic	Performing Adaptations
Enthusiastic - Over-reactor	
Playful - Resister	
Charming - Manipulator	Surviving Adaptations
Brilliant-Sceptic	
Creative - Daydreamer	

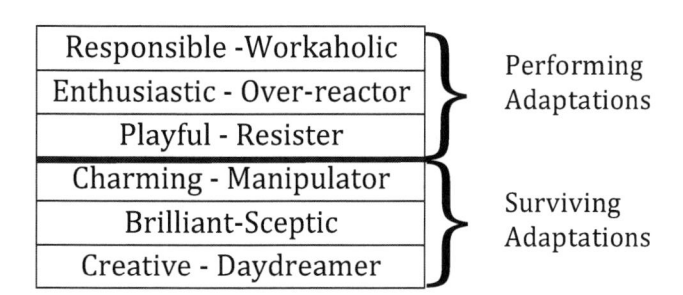

Table 1 Personality Adaptations

Setting Out

the three surviving adaptations, while the three performing adaptations above the line point to their pre-conscious nature.

The Types we Favour

We said earlier on that in order to adapt to life we have all of the adaptations in our repertoire. However, it is generally held that we favour one of the surviving adaptations more than the others. So, we may prefer to withdraw or be sceptical or manipulative in our attempts to survive. Or we may want to show ourselves as creative, brilliant or charming in dealing with survival issues and getting our needs met.

We can, on the other hand, have more than one performing adaptation, but again we frequently favour one of them. It is rare for anyone to have the three performing adaptations in equal measure.

In subsequent chapters we will describe in detail how each of the adaptations develops and under what circumstances. For the moment though we just want to get used to grouping them into the surviving and performing combinations.

Recognising Performing Personality Types

Generally speaking, it is often easier to identify the performing adaptations than the surviving ones, as the performing adaptations are the ones that people demonstrate in the course of a day, and where they engage their performing adaptation(s) in order to gain the recognition and acceptance of others. For example, some people are responsible and work inordinately hard because they believe that in doing so, they gain the admiration of others. Other people are enthusiastic and somewhat over-reactive to liven up a group and reveal themselves as the life and soul of the party. Others, on the other hand, are playful and easy-going to offset the rigidity of the over-controlling boss or partner. Each person will assume a favourite adaptation because as children they gained acceptance by so doing.

Recognizing Surviving Personality Types

What about the surviving adaptations? These seem to become more visible when people are under stress and feel that things are a matter of life and death. So, when the normal performing adaptations do not seem to be working sufficiently well, and the person feels under threat, the surviving adaptations are employed to offset the perceived danger to a person's survival or wellbeing.

Once we have identified the particular surviving and performing adaptations of people, the challenge is to be able to communicate well with them.

The Three Doors of Communication

Paul Ware, the psychiatrist, mentioned in the previous Chapter, devised a model of communication that he found helpful in dealing with the various personalities with whom he had to deal (Ware, 1983:11-19).

He maintained that in order to communicate with a person, we need to be aware that each person has three doors in their personal 'house', doors that allow the person to enter into communication with others. He described these doors as the open door, the target door, and the trapdoor.

The idea of the doors is that in order to connect with a

Setting Out

person, we need first to approach the person's open door. This is the door the person is willing to keep ajar in order to let people in. The target door and the trapdoors are not yet open.

The Open Door
The open door is the first way to connect with a person. Unless they invite us into their 'house' we certainly won't be able to communicate with them

The Target Door
Once inside the 'house' of the person, we can then move to their target door, which they may allow us to open.

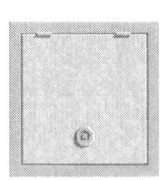

The Trapdoor
This is the secret or private part of the person that they do not want you to access. Don't go there!

Fig 1. The Doors of Communication

Therefore, to approach someone and seek to open the target door or the trapdoor without coming in through the open door will only lead to the person considering the other seeking entry with some hostility. Hence, they will shut down. We need, therefore, to enter by the open door (Fig. 1 above).

Having entered by the open door, we can then safely approach or focus on the so-called target door. Once the target door is open, we do not need to go any further as the person will then be more willing to allow their trapdoor to be opened. However, there is no way a person will allow the trapdoor to open until the thresholds of open door and the target door have been crossed.

Feeling, Thinking and Behaving Doors

Each door has a name on it. There is the thinking door, the feeling door and the behaving door. For some people their open door is their feelings. Therefore, in order to connect with this person, we need to connect with their emotions. If we try to reason with them or worse seek to change their behaviour, we are on a hiding to nothing. They simply will not listen either to our reasons or to our suggestions as to what they should do. Unless we can first connect with them emotionally, they simply will not heed us. So, their target door and trapdoors remain firmly shut.

For another personality, their open door may be their thinking. Hence, if I begin explore their feelings, I will soon find that I am getting nowhere because I am not beginning with their open door . Whatever hope we may have of reaching their target door, we will have no hope of opening their trapdoor if the trapdoor is their feeling

Setting Out

door. So, if we want to connect with someone whose open door is thinking, we need to engage the thinking part of the person before we begin to think about his or her target door.

OPEN → TARGET → TRAP

OPEN	TARGET	TRAP
B	F	T
F	T	B
T	F	B
B	F	T
B	T	F
T	F	B

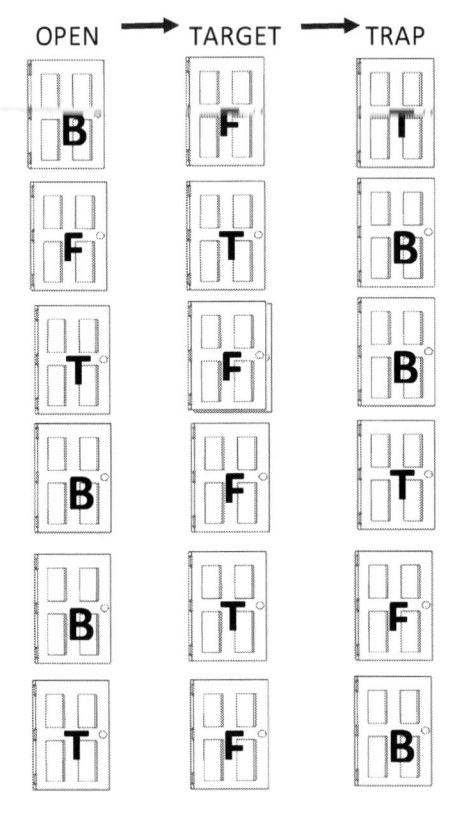

Fig. 2. Open, Target and Trapdoors

By way of completion, when we think of the person whose open door is behaviour, we can only reach that person by engaging with their behaviour. Talking about feelings with them will be met with resistance, and engaging their thinking will only lead to circular argumentation that gets nowhere. Until their behaviour is acknowledged, their thinking and feelings are guarded.

Don't Talk to the Wall!

So, if we look at the various combinations of open door, target door and trapdoor we have the diagram (Fig. 2) as outlined above.

You will notice that some of the combinations are the same. That is because different personality types have the same sequence for people to connect with them. While the sequence is identical, we will later see, however, that the content involved in the thinking, feeling and behaving doors for each adaptation is different. So, while we see two groups with a BFT sequence and two with a TFB sequence, the behaviours, feelings and thinking are not the same for both personality types

Moving from One Door to the Other

Any personality adaptation has the combination of open door, target door and trapdoor and the combination of the three doors goes to define the nature of the personality. By responding to the person according to their preferred channels of communication, we can connect with them effectively.

The main thing to remember is that in order to connect with the various personality adaptations, we need to honour their uniqueness and only seek to approach them through the open doors (thinking, feeling or behaving) for which they have a preference. Therefore, we move along the line of the arrows as shown above, going from open door to target door and finally to the trapdoor. Some people are of the opinion that treating people as subjects with open, target and trapdoors, and interacting with them according to specific sequences smacks of manipulation. They ask, 'Can we not simply take people as they are, and interact in a natural way?'

Setting Out

Why can we not be spontaneous and react to people in a normal way? The question of manipulation needs to be answered.

Is this Manipulation?

Manipulation only occurs when we begin to use our knowledge of the theory to get what we want from people in indirect and secretive ways. It involves taking advantage of the other person's lack of knowledge of their own personality types for our own benefit. Using this model to gain an upper hand would be a cynical manoeuvre that undermines the value of this approach to understanding people.

I am more of the opinion that when we fully understand the other person, and interact according to their preferred open door, we are honouring their uniqueness and responding to their needs in a respectful way. This is far from manipulation.

Conclusion

This chapter has outlined the essential elements of the theory of personality adaptations or types. We have seen that the very bases for this typology are the behaviours that children unconsciously adopt in order to overcome the challenges of survival. Then, these same children have to adapt again in order to feel accepted by their parents and the society in which they live. This two-fold adaptation leads to the formation of the personality types – surviving and performing types.

Each type is characterised by the three doors of thinking, feeling and behaving, and each personality type will have its own specific sequence which we will see when describing them in Chapters 5 to 10.

In the next Chapter we will link the personality types with the theory of Transactional Analysis so as to offer a clear theoretical basis for this approach to personality differences. Originally, this model of personality types was developed by Transactional Analysts and the combination of TA and the personality types go hand-in-hand to create a rich theory of personality.

CHAPTER THREE

An Essential Ingredient

*"No matter what the recipe,
any baker can do wonders in the kitchen
with some good ingredients and an upbeat attitude!"*
Buddy Valastro

Eric Berne (1910-1970) was the originator of Transactional Analysis, which he devised in reaction to the overly long and potentially expensive psychoanalytic therapy that was in vogue at the time. His belief was that a patient could be cured in one session as opposed to someone undergoing therapy for years. While his claim for such a rapid solution to a person's problems can be taken with a pinch of salt, Berne did offer a form of therapy that was more accessible to the ordinary person.

The four principal ingredients of TA involve ego state analysis, transactional analysis, game analysis and Script analysis. Each of these components combines to create an impressive and coherent theory of personality, of communication and of psychopathology.

In this book we will focus on ego state analysis (one of the ingredients) as it is this aspect of Berne's work that is especially useful in understanding the dynamics of personality adaptations. For people who wish to pursue Berne's theory more deeply, I have offered a more extensive explanation in *Why Are We Together?* and at the end of *Don't Talk to the Wall!* I offer a selection of books that deal with TA in a more detailed fashion. However, in order to understand personality types, the reader does not need an in-depth understanding of Transactional Analysis. Nevertheless, it is useful to see what Berne meant by ego states as this idea fits well with the theory of personality types.

What Are Ego States?

Eric Berne defined an ego state as 'a consistent pattern of thinking and experience directly related to a corresponding consistent pattern of behaviour.' (Berne, 1966:364). What he was highlighting was that within us there are a number of personalities each with thoughts, feelings and behaviours that influence the way we see ourselves, others and the world.

The three ego states Berne identified were the Parent, Adult and Child ego states. He used capital letters for each personality to distinguish them from parents, adults and children in general.

The Parent Ego State

The Parent ego state develops from a person's experience of their own parents and parent figures, and where they hold the memory of these influences inside themselves, often finding themselves thinking, feeling and behaving just like their parents did in the past. So, when we say that a person is in their Parent ego state we mean that they are acting like their own parents. The Parent ego state is, therefore, different for each person since we each have the experience of our own parents.

The Adult Ego State

Just as the Parent ego state includes the thinking, feeling and behaving elements of the ego state, so the Adult ego state equally uses thinking, feeling and behaviour in response to the current reality that confronts the person. Whereas the Parent ego state refers to the past, the Adult is in the present, responding to the here-and-now reality. The Adult is that ego state that we seek to have more dominant in our lives because it offers us the best way of dealing with life.

The Child Ego State

The Child ego state comprises the thinking, feeling and behaviours that people experienced when they were children. Like the Parent ego state, the Child ego state comes from the past of the person and is unique to that individual. No person's Child ego state is the same as another person's, just as no Parent ego state of a person is exactly the same as another person's. Even among siblings, the Parent and Child ego states are not identical because each person experiences their parents and their childhood in a unique way.

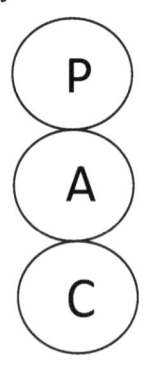

Fig. 3 The Ego State Model (Berne, 1961)

Don't Talk to the Wall!

Berne diagrammed the ego states by placing three circles in the order of Parent, Adult and Child as in Fig. 3 above. This diagram demonstrates the reality of our way of being in the three ego states. Our Adult is in the middle to show that it can be influenced from either the Parent or the Child.

Contamination of the Adult

Sometimes we may think we are being in Adult when in reality we are thinking, feeling and/or behaving from a Child or Parent ego state. When this happens we are in a situation where our Adult is being contaminated (Berne, 1961:47). If we were to diagram the contaminations, they would look like Fig. 4.

| Parent | Child | Double |
| Contamination | Contamination | Contamination |

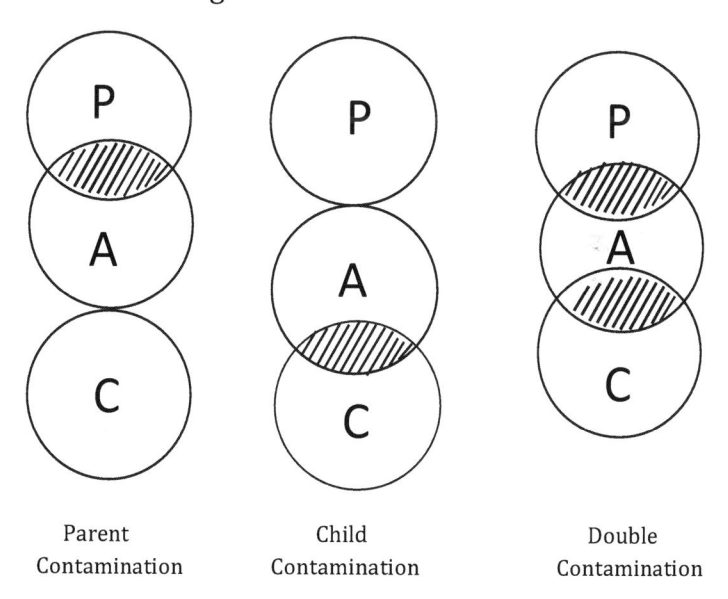

Fig. 4 Contaminations (Berne, 1961)

Parent Contamination

When people think they are in Adult and are contaminated by a Parent ego state, they will often reveal

25

prejudices and opinions that are rigid, moralistic and critical. They will see themselves in a one-up position, and are only too ready to persecute, control or demean the other person. When asked if they think they are acting as an adult, they would strongly insist that they are.

Child Contamination

A Child ego state contamination can be evidenced in the person who expresses childhood fears and fantasies that have more to do with their past than with the current reality. Alternatively, the person may demonstrate childish characteristics that seem rather inappropriate to their adult status. Like the adult who believes he or she is acting from their Adult ego state while obviously displaying Child ego state thoughts, feelings and behaviours, often the person is unaware of what ego state is in force at specific moments or under certain circumstances. It is only when people begin to identify their fears and doubts that they come to see that they are not in their Adult but are dominated by their Child.

Double Contamination

A double contamination from the Parent and Child ego states means that the amount of Adult available to the person is seriously compromised. Looking at the diagram of double contamination, we see that quite a considerable amount of the Adult space is being taken up with the prejudices of the Parent and the scares/delusions of the child. So, with a double contamination there is usually an inner battle going on between a Controlling or Critical Parent that is seeking to persecute the Child ego state, and the Child ego state is either caving in to the demands of the Parent, or stubbornly refusing to accede to the wishes of the Parent. With this internal conflict, the Adult finds itself torn between the contradicting and bewildering voices of the Parent and the Child ego states.

Contaminations and Personality Types

When we begin to classify the various personality adaptations, we will see that each adaptation is characterised by differing levels of contamination. Some of the adaptations will have a Parent contamination, while others will either have a Child contamination or a combination of Parent and Child contamination. Understanding the idea of contaminations offers the person a level of insight into what they need to do to counter the contamination from whatever quarter it arises.

Finally, it is useful to look at the behaviours of the Parent, Adult and Child that are in each of us, and which can be clearly identified in the way we speak or act or even by our posture.

How Ego States Function

The functional ego state model devised by Eric Berne identifies the behaviours of the person when they are in Parent, or Adult or Child (Berne, 1961:154). So, when a person is in Parent, they will act either in a controlling or critical way, or in a nurturing way (Fig. 5 overleaf). When the person is in Child they can be either in their spontaneous or Free Child ego state, or they have to adapt by being a Conforming Child (CC) or a Rebellious Child (RC). The Adult from the diagram overleaf represents that part of the person that acts in the here–and-now.

An Essential Ingredient

Depending on the levels of contamination which we discussed above, our way of acting and interacting with others will be strongly influenced, leading us to behave from a Parent, Adult or Child ego state.

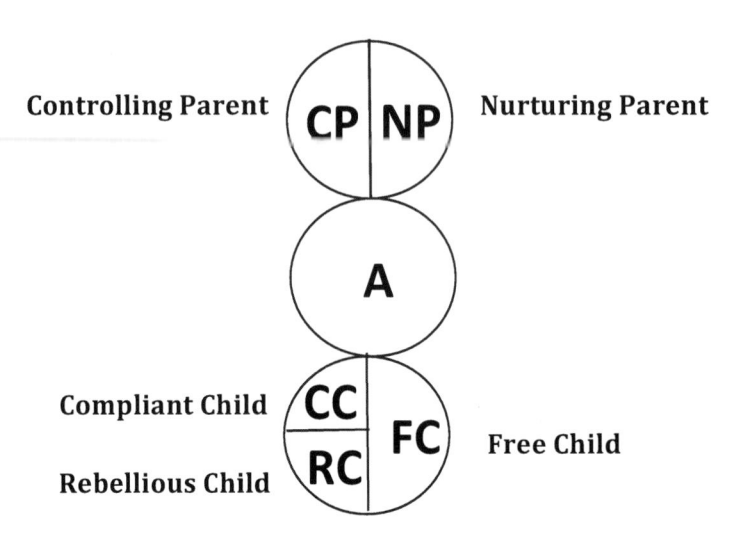

Controlling Parent CP | NP **Nurturing Parent**

A

Compliant Child CC
Rebellious Child RC | FC **Free Child**

Fig. 5 The Functional Model of Ego States (based on Drye 1974)

How Contaminations Come About

In the next Chapter we examine how such contaminations occur. Invariably, they are the result of conscious and unconscious messages sent by parents to their children in the course of the child's development. For the sake of clarity and simplicity, we limit our discussion to exploring the conscious and verbal messages sent by parents to their children, and which have a significant impact on the way the child learns to behave. While the unconscious messages sent by parents to their children are equally influential in determining how a person will grow and develop, in this instance we are more interested in the external behaviour of the individual, and how this behaviour is linked inextricably with the various personality adaptations.

In addition, it may also be important to mention that children are also influenced by other family members, caregivers other than parents, teachers, church ministers and indeed the wider cultural environment into which they child is introduced. This is not to lessen the significant influence of parents, but rather to acknowledge the fact that many factors are involved in the creation of the personality of the child.

Conclusion

The idea of ego states offers us a useful way to understand the internal messages that are continually going on in our heads in the course of a day. It is useful to begin to become aware of these voices and to identify from whence they come. Are they the voices of our parents who were critical, controlling or nurturing? What happens when we make mistakes or find ourselves failing in some way? Are we gentle with ourselves, or harsh and unforgiving like our parents may have been?

Alternatively, are we conscious of a child tape playing away in our heads, filling us with a sense of fear, or sadness or playfulness?

Maybe, on the other hand, we hear a measured, mature and balanced voice that comes from our Adult ego state, and which seems to be able to face both moments of success and failure with a certain equanimity.

Recognising which voice predominates is the beginning of understanding personality adaptations and how they develop from our earliest years.

CHAPTER FOUR

Conditional Love

> "If my love is without sacrifice, it is selfish. Such a love is barter, for there is exchange of love and devotion in return for something. It is conditional love."
> Sadhu Vaswani

When children are born they become all powerful for the first couple of years. All being well, they have their mothers and fathers at their beck and call. When they are hungry, or uncomfortable or just lonely or frightened all they have to do is cry or shout, and the mother or father comes running to feed, clean or simply comfort them. These children learn early on how to gain the attention of their caregivers, and feel confident that their needs will be met as soon as they are expressed. Sadly, this is not the case for all children as some are not welcomed into the world, and may be neglected or abandoned.

The Disillusionment of Childhood

With the passing of years children come to realize that the parents are not so attentive or willing to be their offspring's personal slaves. Children see that when they want something, the parents begin to set down boundaries and even refuse at times to accede to what they want.

Even worse, children gradually begin to feel that their parents are not always as unconditionally loving as they thought they were initially. It gradually dawns on them that this love that they thought was in endless supply is, in fact, a commodity that will have to be earned in some way. They cannot depend on it coming automatically and this gradual realization often engenders feelings of fear and rage as they begin to understand that they are no longer the kings and queens of the castle! At the same time, there is still the strong need to depend on their parents for the children's existence. They cannot dismiss their parents and look for more accommodating adults. These are the only adults they have.

Love is not Unconditional

Nor can the children blame their parents openly for fear that their parents will abandon them. This fear of abandonment will not necessarily be a conscious awareness, but even so, lurking in the unconscious is a primitive terror that they could be rejected, orphaned or even annihilated either physically or emotionally. Therefore, children begin to understand that the love they initially thought was unconditional love is, in fact, conditional with clear demands attached to its supply.

In response to this dawning awareness, children begin to rebel, screaming and shouting in protest at the unfairness of these restrictions to what they originally thought was a birth-given right. Alternatively, they go into a form of depression, lamenting the withdrawal of the endless supply of parental affection. Some children may simply go into a state of numbness where they kill off all the feelings they had so as not to experience the

Conditional Love

disappointment and panic at the loss of their source of affection. This can occur around the age of two to three. But for the most part children learn to adapt to the changing situation by developing *drivers.*

What are Drivers?

After the initial shock that unconditional love does not exist, children's clever Little Professor (their Adult ego state when they were a child) works out a way to earn affection, or if not affection then simple acceptance from their parents. This process of adapting to the parent's conditional love leads to children developing what Taibi Kahler called *driver behaviour* (Kahler, 1978).

Kahler maintained that in response to the parents withdrawal of unconditional love, children pick up the clear message that, if they are to be acceptable at home, they have to behave in specific ways. In addition, because children want so much to be loved and accepted, they will feel pressurized or driven to adopt certain behaviours that will guarantee the continued affection they so need from their parents. The five *drivers* that Kahler identified were: *Be Perfect, Be Strong, Please Others, Try Hard* and *Hurry Up* (Kahler, 1978: 243). A word of explanation on each driver will contribute to our understanding of personality types.

The Drivers

Be Perfect
Be Strong
Try Hard
Please Others
Hurry Up

Be Perfect

Children who develop a *Be Perfect* driver often come from homes where the parents demand of their children that they reach high standards in all they do. The parents will be highly critical of their children, never satisfied unless their children are matching up to an impossible ideal set by them. Indeed, the ideals never seem to be clearly identified, and children discover that no matter how perfectly they complete a task, it never seems to fully satisfy their parents.

As a result of this continual demand for excellence on the part of parents, children begin to internalize the uncompromising demands for excellence by the parents, and gradually assume that critical voice in their own Parent ego state. This is a good example of the Parent contamination that we discussed in the last Chapter. Children develop an internal critical voice that continually harps on the perfection that they never succeed in achieving.

When children then grow into adults, this same internal Parental voice continues to persecute the grown-up person, filling their heads with an inner recording of their original parents that never permits them to settle for a 'good-enough' job. They have to strive unceasingly to be better, more perfect, more upright etc. never allowing them to relax and take a break. This is the *Be Perfect* driver.

Recognizing the Be Perfect

It is fairly easy to recognize someone with a *Be Perfect* driver. Usually they come across in their dress and comportment as perfect in every way. They dress tastefully with nothing out of place and often colour coordinated in subtle ways. They are usually immaculately groomed and orderly in the way they keep their surroundings. When they speak, they try to ensure that nothing is omitted from what they want to say. Consequently, they will frequently clarify each statement they make, using many parentheses and sub-clauses so that they have included all aspects of their argument. Their movements will be carefully controlled and you will frequently see them steepling their fingers as they talk, often counting on their fingers the various points they want to make. They are highly sensitive to criticism, and will go to any length to explain away their mistakes.

Be Strong
Children who develop a *Be Strong* driver usually come from homes where parents seem to send a message to their children that feelings are *verboten*. When children express strong emotions in these situations, the parents cannot cope with their children's feelings, and either ignore their expression or positively dissuade their children from any emotional displays. Besides the parental ban on crying, these parents look with distain or unease on any spontaneous expressions of positive or negative feelings. The parents feel more comfortable when their children don't feel at all!

As a result, the parents only accept their children when they are in control of their emotions. Their love is conditional on the capacity of their children to contain feelings and refrain from any exaggerated display of affect.

As these children grow into adulthood, they in turn incorporate this injunction not to feel that as children they picked up from their parents. Consequently, they now live their lives within the narrow confines of an emotionally controlled environment. Anything that will upset them, they avoid, and they are more comfortable when their emotional continuum is restricted.

Recognizing the Be Strong

Adults who have a *Be Strong* driver usually appear to be controlled and guarded in both posture and speech. They talk in a rather monotone fashion without much modulation that would express any trace of emotional highs or lows. They will often sit with their arms folded as if to hold themselves together, and you will see them covering their mouths as if they want to hide any indication of feeling that they think will be revealed in that part of the body. In the way they speak, they objectify emotions by talking *about* emotions rather than feeling them. They will say something like, "It was an unhappy situation," instead of saying, "I was unhappy." Or, they will blame others or the situation for the feelings they have. So, they will put the responsibility on others for their feelings: 'He made me angry." Or they will point to a situation describing it as 'boring', instead of saying, "I was bored." Feelings for them are 'things' rather than emotional states that they experience first hand, that is if they feel anything at all. Some are so cut off from their feelings that they do not even recognize any physical sensations in their body.

Try Hard

The person with the *Try Hard* driver is likely to have come from a family situation where the parents were

Conditional Love

perceived by the child as over-controlling. When the child starts to feel that the parents are too domineering, the child begins the power struggle and refuses to give in. Initially the battle may be played out on the potty, where the child can refuse to cooperate with the parents with regard to toilet training. This lack of cooperation then develops and increases with the corresponding attempts of the parents to direct their child in a particular direction. Often this rebellion is not a loud or bloody battle, but more like a silent revolution that is characterized by a type of passive aggression.

Often in this situation, the parents settle for less, affirming their child for having tried to complete a task. They seem to capitulate in the battle for wills, and content themselves when their child *tries* to achieve some objective. In a sense, the parents have given up on their children, willing to accept that effort is at least something that is worthy of praise. Children, on their part, come to understand the messages from their parents that tell them that they are OK as long as they try. They don't have to succeed in order to gain acceptance. In a sense, they are motivated to mediocrity!

Recognizing the Try Hard

People with a *Try Hard* driver are seen to be trying hard. They seem to strain and stress in attempting to complete a task. Life for them seems to be a struggle, and they often complain that they have too much to do, or that they are tired having done what they had to do, even though the task was not that onerous. They sometimes seem to be deaf, straining to hear what the other person is saying, and often expressing that they do not understand what the person is trying to communicate.

As this child grows into adulthood he or she seems content when they have *tried* to do a job or task. You will often hear them say, 'I'll try to...' instead of saying, 'I'll do that.' Often they never do what they said they would *try* to do. In addition, they often leave things undone or they postpone arranged meetings much to the frustration of those around them.

Please Others

People with the *Please Others* drivers seek literally to please anyone with whom they come in contact. They often smile a lot, almost flirting with the person to show they want to make the person happy. You will often see them with their heads slightly looking downwards while their eyes are looking upward in an attempt to show a slightly fawning attitude. They simply love feeling that they are making the other person happy. When others are pleased, they are content.

Adults who develop a *Please Others* driver often come from families where they, as children, were spoilt. They may have been the mother or father's pet. They entered into an almost incestuous closeness with one or both parents, where they felt the compulsion to please their parents and in turn experienced the parents' love and affection.

Recognizing the Please Others

People with a *Please Others* driver will often be seen to smile a lot, seeking to connect with people and showing their teeth in a sort of grimace that is more of a strained smile. Frequently they seem to lower their heads and look upwards to people in a sort of fawning way.

In their language, they are inclined to use words like: 'gee!' and 'gosh' when expressing pleasure or surprise, instead of expressing themselves in a more adult way.

Often they will be inclined to 'smother' people, offering to do things for others even when no help is requested. They become the classic rescuers who discount the capacity for others to solve their own problems. They are continually alert to the needs and wants of those around them and take particular delight in being helpful. In fact, they are only happy when they are helping since the *Please Others* driver is their preferred and compulsive way of being.

Hurry Up

Children who grew up in a family 'on the move' could easily develop a *Hurry Up* driver. Their parents were not able to enjoy their children as they naturally moved through childhood and adolescence, but were always eager for their children to achieve something immediately. Patience was not a feature of the parents' approach to life. Their timetable was action-packed, and instead of being able to take it easy and accomplish things in an orderly fashion, they created an atmosphere of agitation and panic.

Their children picked up this frenetic pace and, as a result, when these children grew into adulthood, they followed in the footsteps of their parents, always feeling pressurized by whatever tasks they undertook. Rather than take their time to achieve a satisfactory result, those with the *Hurry Up* driver are more interested in the destination than in the journey. In their anxiety to reach the final destination, they speed along the path of life, failing to enjoy the people and events they meet on the way, and thereby living at a very superficial level. Instead of connecting with people, they rush from once person to the next without any real contact.

Recognizing the Hurry Up

These adults only feel OK when they are on the move, and are impatient with themselves and others if results are not immediately obvious.

One of the main characteristics of those with the *Hurry Up* driver is their difficulty in really listening to other people. In their impatience, they seek to finish other people's sentences either aloud by interrupting them, or internally where they presume to know what people are saying and then simply respond to what they supposedly heard. In their haste, they fail to pick up what is actually being said.

Are Drivers always negative?

Much of the description that I have given of *driver* behaviour sounds very negative. What is wrong with trying hard or pleasing others? There is no doubt great value in people working hard, pleasing others, having some control of their emotional highs and lows, getting things right, and not wasting time. These are the more positive aspects of the drivers. What needs to be kept in mind, however, is that when we talk of *drivers* we are focusing on the compulsive nature of the behaviours, which in normal circumstances would otherwise be positive aspects of a person's way of living. When a person is under the influence of a driver, they are not free but are feeling pressurized to be a certain way. Putting it another way, they will find it difficult to please themselves, or take their time or do things to a certain level of accuracy without having to be perfect.

Contaminations, Drivers and Personality Adaptations

Both contaminations and drivers contribute to the mechanism of forming personality adaptations. As the young person incorporates both the parent messages and their unconscious reactions to these distorted parental communications, the child learns to adapt in order to 'fit in' to the family system.

The motive for any adaptation is to gain the love and acceptance of the parents, and early on in life, children realize that love is rarely unconditional.

Parents are not to Blame

It should be understood that the parents' reaction to their children comes from their own struggles going back to their childhood. Their somewhat unconscious reaction to the behaviours of their children plays out their need for inner control. In trying to control their children, they are attempting to manage their own struggles and deal with their past history (Holloway, 1972:32-34). Hence, their inability to offer unconditional love to their children need not be seen as a criticism of parents but rather as a way to understand why parents react the way they do to their children.

The Six Personality Adaptations or Types

The stage is now set for us to examine in detail the six personality adaptations that we learn as we move from childhood to adulthood. In each of the personality adaptation profiles we will outline their main characteristics, and offer some suggestions as to how they developed. We will point to the driver messages linked to each of the adaptations, and also indicate what sorts of contaminations are characteristic in each case.

We will also indicate how best to communicate with each of the personality adaptations, and how people can develop a more holistic type of adaptation to offset the unhealthy elements of their personality adaptation.

In Chapters 5-7, we will describe the three surviving personality adaptations first, since these are the ones that develop very early in a child's life. Then in Chapters 8 to 10, we will describe the performing adaptations.

Are We Talking about Personality Disorders?

In their extreme form, the personality adaptations can be classified as personality disorders. In some of the writing on personality adaptations, in fact, authors use the clinical titles for each adaptation: Creative Daydreamer (Schizoid Personality Disorder), Brilliant Sceptic (Paranoid Personality Disorder), Charming Manipulator (Antisocial Personality Disorder), Responsible Workaholic (Obsessive-Compulsive Disorder), Enthusiastic Over-reactor (Histrionic Personality Disorder), and the Playful Resister (Passive-Aggressive Disorder). The personality types parallel the psychopathological terms used when a person displays the personality types in their extreme form. I think, however, that the work of Joines and Stewart offers a more descriptive classification of the various types (Joines & Stewart, 2002). What I particularly like about these more friendly descriptions of the various adaptations is that they include both the positive and less positive dimensions of each character type, and thereby offer a glimpse into the values that each personality type enshrines.

These alternative descriptions also serve to underline the fact that we are not describing disorders, but rather ways in which we all adapt to our environment.

Disorder or Adaptation?	
Schizoid	Creative Daydreamer
Paranoid	Brilliant Sceptic
Antisocial	Charming Manipulator
Obsessive Compulsive	Responsible Workaholic
Histrionic	Enthusiastic Over-Reactor
Passive Aggressive	Playful Resister

At the beginning of the following Chapters dealing with the various personality adaptations, you will notice the graphic showing the open, target and trapdoors with the relevant label of thinking, feeling or behaviour attached to each of the specific doors. This provides a key to each of the personality types, and should help the reader in focusing on the specific dynamics of each personality.

Again, I want to acknowledge the valuable work of Vann Joines and Ian Stewart whose book on Personality Adaptations forms the basis for the various descriptions of the personality types (Joines & Stewart, 2002).

The Creative Daydreamer

CHAPTER FIVE

The Creative Daydreamer

"I don't think there's any artist of any value who doesn't doubt what they're doing."
Francis Ford Coppola

John hates parties. He goes along simply because his wife Mary drags him kicking and screaming so to speak because she doesn't want to be there alone. She is also worried that John is becoming more of a recluse. But John isn't a party animal. He goes along but as soon as he can, he slips out of their friend's house to light up a cigarette, but mainly to get away from the constant chatter of his wife's friends. He can't understand how they can spend the whole evening chatting about 'stuff'. Occasionally Michael, the husband, joins him from the partying crowd, but John is quite happy if no one joins him. He likes being alone.

Of course, he can't stay outside all night, so he returns

to the noisy chatter, and sits there pretending to listen to the non-stop stories and gossip interspersed with laughter and hilarity. He often fixes his attention on the picture on the wall, wondering why they chose that particular painting, which he finds strange and uninteresting. It looks like a chocolate box cover to him. They could have got a lovely reproduction of Picasso, he thinks.

On the way home he is happy to listen to Mary as she shares on the wonderful time she had. Mary knows John dreads parties, but she was really appreciative that he came. Even though John had reluctantly gone to the party, he was happy that Mary had enjoyed herself.

The thing John really likes doing is taking care of the garden and studying everything to do with flowers. That is so relaxing and he loves it. He can be alone with his thoughts and feelings as he potters among his prized roses. Sometimes he wonders what Mary sees in going to parties, and yet somewhere inside John is a sense that he is losing out on something, and he is aware that he is a loner and realizes that he doesn't really have many friends.

A Clinical Picture

Creative Daydreamers (the traditional schizoid personality) grew up in a family where they perceived that their parents were not really willing or able to manage the various tasks involved in childrearing. From an early age, this child saw the mother as not really capable of being a competent mother, and the father appeared somewhat disconnected from the child's world. In some cases, the mother and father both work and do not seem to be able to balance the time given to their careers and the time needed to care for their children. The perception on the part of the child that the parents are not present may have had a basis in reality, or it may simply have been the child's view of his or her situation.

Whatever the reality of the matter was, the child makes an early decision to take care of him or herself. The child therefore withdraws inside into the fantasy world that is infinitely more attractive to the apparent lack of security without. It is in this world that the child finds comfort and safety. John is a good example of such a personality.

It is within this world of fantasy and self-soothing that the child becomes wonderfully creative. Nothing is impossible in the private world of a child, and so as the child grows up, he or she develops the creative right brain activity that favours the poetic, the artistic and the somewhat self-absorbed.

Recognizing Creative Daydreamers

Often Creative Daydreamers come across as rather shy and withdrawn, happy to be in their own company, and inclined to avoid close personal contact with others. They can be seen as rather detached emotionally, and often can be caught daydreaming and in another world. For John, daydreaming is a pleasurable activity!

Sometimes Creative Daydreamers can appear somewhat eccentric or unique in their way of living, but usually in a gentle and intriguing way. Gentleness is an attractive side of their personality.

Often Creative Daydreamers also display a melancholic side to them, seemingly in touch with sadness and, at times, bordering on feelings of depression. The feelings of sadness are often a substitute for more authentic feelings of anger at the way they were treated as children. However, since expressing anger was not encouraged when they were children, Creative Daydreamers develop the 'substitute feeling' of sadness (English, 1972: 23-25; 1978:78-81).

The Drivers

The Creative Daydreamer's main *driver* is *Be Strong*. As we saw when discussing drivers in Chapter 4, we can presume that the Creative Daydreamer personality adaptation emerged from an environment where parents seemed to send a message to their children that feelings are not to be expressed freely. When children expressed strong emotions in these situations, the parents could not cope and either ignored their expression, or positively dissuaded their children from any emotional displays. The parents sent the injunction to their child that they should not feel. Consequently, Creative Daydreamers only feel comfortable when they are in control of their feelings or out of touch with them.

As Creative Daydreamers grow into adulthood they, in turn, incorporate this injunction from their parents not to feel, and live their lives within the narrow confines of an emotionally controlled environment.

Creative Daydreamers who have a *Be Strong* driver usually appear to be emotionally restricted and measured in both posture and speech. They talk in a rather monotone fashion without much modulation to express any trace of emotional highs or lows. As we mentioned in Chapter 4, Creative Daydreamers with the *Be Strong* driver will often hold themselves in a rather controlled manner as if they are conscious of their bodies, and of the need to be in control of their movements. They avoid any exuberant displays of emotion and appear to want to fade into the background. When talking about something that interests or enthuses them they will use more objective language rather than personal expressions of delight or pleasure. So, for instance, they might say that gardening is a very pleasant pastime as was the case with John, instead of saying, 'I really love gardening.'

It would be a mistake, however, to think that the Creative Daydreamers do not feel. In fact, they have strong feelings that often emerge in their poetry, their art or in their fantasy, or in John's case in tending to his garden. Their feelings are present in their private world. The main challenge facing them is to be able to express their feelings openly. However, since they experienced the injunction not to feel, they hide their feelings under the trapdoor of their private life.

In general, Creative Daydreamers are inclined to be more passive than active. When they are part of a team, they seldom volunteer to do a job. They simply prefer to wait until they are asked to do something instead of actively engaging in a group activity. At times, they may be seen as non-cooperative and lazy, but in reality they are simply living within their personal bubble, and are waiting to be invited out so as to actively engage in a project. They can stay in this passive state for indefinite periods, or until they are invited to undertake some responsibility.

Contaminations

From a contamination point of view, the Creative

Don't Talk to the Wall!

daydreamer's Adult is affected by various injunctions from their parents. Often they have picked up messages not to feel or be close to people. They may have been discouraged to belong, and certainly they were not encouraged to allow their emotions to be expressed. The contamination from their early Child ego state related to their scare in the face of the belief that their parents were not able to cope well. Hence, the belief that they had to withdraw and avoid putting any demands on their parents, led the Creative Daydreamer to believe that they had to take care of themselves. The Creative Daydreamer goes through life with the contaminated belief that they have to go it alone. Because they have been on their own for most of their lives, Creative Daydreamers are comfortable spending long periods of time in their own company. Seldom do they feel lonely, and often they can develop a taste for solitude, which sustains them when they are on their own. In Fig. 6 we see how the contaminations from both Parent and Child scares the Child ego state and causes the Child to flee into the privacy of solitude.

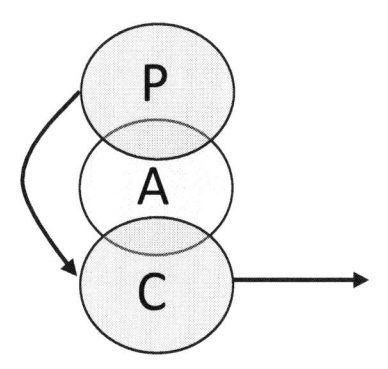

Fig. 6 The Withdrawal of the Creative Daydreamer
(based on Joines & Stewart, 2002)

The Doors of Communication

The open door of the Creative Daydreamer is through behaviour. Because this personality adaptation favours withdrawal as their preferred behaviour, the challenge in communicating with them is to invite them out of their private world. In order to get a message through to them we need to be more directive in our invitation. So, in talking with them we need to say something like. 'Mary, help me with this job I'm doing.' This rather directive approach would be resisted with other personality types, but with the Creative Daydreamer they need to hear a clear invitation or a clear command to bring them out of their passivity. Once we get them to move, then we can direct our attention to their target door. The target door of the Creative Daydreamer opens to their thinking. So, when we want to know how the Creative Daydreamer is experiencing a situation or an event, it is not helpful to ask them how they are feeling, for feelings lie hidden in their trapdoor. Even if we do ask them how they are feeling, they will come back with something like, "I feel that we should do this quickly." When we say we are feeling *that*, in reality we are thinking. It's only when we put the feeling word immediately after the word 'feeling' that we are expressing authentic emotions! So, when I say, "I'm feeling sad or happy or angry", then I'm sharing my real feelings.

The trapdoor of the Creative Daydreamer is their feelings; so we need to avoid attempting to enter into this secret area of the Creative Daydreamer. When we try to focus on feelings, we will be resisted valiantly. Consequently, the most effective way of communicating with Creative Daydreamers is to invite them out of their withdrawn passivity and then target their thinking, inviting them to engage at a cognitive level. Once we do that, Creative Daydreamers gradually come in contact with their feelings that are hidden under the trapdoor.

In the normal course of the day, Creative Daydreamers move from their withdrawing behaviour to dwell on their emotions without engaging their thinking. But this focus on feelings is private and not available to others. They are in a private emotional and usually melancholic world of their own. It is only when they are invited out of their inner world, and their thinking is engaged by the other party, that Creative Daydreamers can access a wider emotional repertoire, and then begin to communicate their authentic feelings. Time and patience is needed for this to happen.

As we said previously, you will find below a number of statements that the Creative Daydreamer might hold. By indicating which ones apply to you, you may have some idea as to whether your surviving adaptation is the Creative Daydreamer. Following each of the personality types that follow, you will find other corresponding statements for your consideration.

The Creative Daydreamer

Beliefs or Statements of the Creative Daydreamer

1. I enjoy my own company and seldom feel lonely.

2. I often find it difficult to know what I'm feeling when people ask me how I feel.

3. I am happier talking to one or two people rather than with a crowd.

4. I seldom volunteer my thoughts and feelings unless I'm invited to share them.

5. Generally I don't experience highs or lows in my emotions.

6. I don't like people who are overly emotional.

7. I prefer to be told what to do rather than be left to decide for myself.

8. I'm more a team player than a leader, although I prefer to be left alone and get on with the job-in-hand rather than have to work with others.

9. I prefer the other person to take the initiative when keeping in touch with friends.

10. When I feel down or depressed I seldom share this with other, preferring to manage on my own.

11. I find it easier to feel sad and disappointed than to feel angry.

Count the number of the statements or beliefs that you consider true for you. Total: _____

The Brilliant Sceptic

CHAPTER SIX

The Brilliant Sceptic

*"The greatest tragedy with a sceptic
is that he cannot consign himself to truth,
however he may see it."*
Raheel Farooq

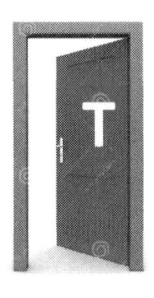

Sheila and Jane sat in Sheila's office as the two of them often did when they wanted to discuss plans for the development of their business. Sheila was really enthusiastic over her ideas for the reorganization of their company. Jane was less so.
- So, Jane, if we build the office block away from the manufacturing plant, it will mean that we can separate the administration from the rest of our activity.
- What good would that do Sheila? Isn't it better to have both combined? (Jane was wondering what Sheila was really up to).

- Well, I thought management was getting in the way of the day-to-day working of manufacturing, and things weren't working out. (Sheila sounded convinced of her plan, but Jane was having none of it).

- What do you mean things aren't working out, Sheila?

- Well, Margaret is always interfering with the foreman's responsibilities, and you know that over the last five years there have been continual rows and disagreements. Anyway, I've decided to make the move, and I hope you'll back me up.

- How much is this entire project going to cost, Sheila? I think the whole plan is mad. And why wasn't I part of this planning?

- It will be money well spent, Jane. We'll have a brand new office where accounts and publicity will join with research and development so that we can have things more streamlined.

- But how much will it cost? Where's the money coming from for God's sake? (Jane was beginning to get frustrated and bewildered).

- Look Jane, you're going to have to trust me on this one. I've spent a lot of time thinking about this restructuring, and I believe that things will work out fine. I have contacted the architects and already they are excited about the project.

Jane was mystified at the whole idea. She wasn't going to agree to this hair-brained scheme of Sheila, even though Sheila was the boss. This plan was going to be a disaster, and Jane felt sure that behind Sheila's plan was an overall strategy to move her sideways. This was not going to happen. She would keep challenging Sheila until she dropped the whole idea. Jane simply could not get it into her head that Sheila was in fact trying simply to improve the running of the operation.

The Clinical Picture

The Brilliant Sceptic personality adaptation, as shown in Jane, reveals elements of paranoid traits. On the one hand, these people show brilliance in their thought processes while, on the other hand, they reveal a suspicious attitude to others and to the world in general. She may have been spot on in her critique of Sheila's plan, but totally wrong in her suspicions as to Sheila's motives.

The Brilliant Sceptic usually develops in a family where there is a high level of unpredictability. It may be that the parents were inconsistent in their way of treating their children. One day the parents are encouraging and supportive, while the next day they are critical and even threatening. This uncertainty disturbs children, leaving them bewildered and anxious about what their parents will be like on any given day. In the face of this unpredictability, these children become experts in reading the signs of the times. They pick up the fluctuations in mood in the family, and work out ways to protect themselves and avoid any fallout in the wake of changes in the home situation.

This personality adaptation can also develop in early life when there is a major deterioration in the circumstances of the family. The death of a parent when the child is in its early years can create a sense of anxiety, leaving the child frightened and unsure as to what the future will bring. One of the parents could have been hospitalised, leaving the child wondering what had happened, and fearful that they may have been to blame for the parent's misfortune. Another scenario, which causes deep anxiety and hyper vigilance, is when there is conflict between the parents, or when one of the parents develops problems with addictions of any sort. The result of such uncertainly is that the child prematurely develops the left side of the cortex – the logical, linguistic and linear qualities of thinking – to help make sense of their situation, instead of allowing the right brain (their emotional and creative side) to fully develop first in an atmosphere of care and security.

Recognising the Brilliant Sceptic

As children grow into adults, their brilliance and scepticism grows. Brilliant Sceptics are noted for their clear thinking and their capacity to unmask any form of deceit. Often they are highly intelligent and razor sharp in identifying flaws or problems in a proposal or plan. It was obvious to Jane that Sheila's plan was badly conceived. Brilliant Sceptics seem to hone in on the weak points of any argument, and then can brilliantly express their critical views. Many a barrister has the qualities of the Brilliant Sceptic! Jane showed her clear thinking as opposed to Sheila's somewhat fuzzy planning.

The paranoid dimension of this personality adaptation also reveals itself in their annoyance when they are not being informed with regard to plans that involve them. They get extremely angry and at times almost aggressive when people do not keep them up to speed on developments that affect them. Their anger really masks a deep-seated fear that they will not be able to manage the changing scenario.

In general it can be said that their most authentic feeling is one of fear, which they often fail to recognise, and instead express a substitute feeling of anger when they are faced with uncertainty.

The Brilliant Sceptic can come across are somewhat rigid or stubborn, and when in an argument, they become tenacious in putting over their ideas to the point, at times, of revealing a certain grandiosity. They are right, and are proud of being right – always!

They can also be hypersensitive, seeing hurts where none was intended, and can attack when they feel they are being slighted. Such sensitivity is often coupled with a high level of suspicion that people are 'out to get them'.

Finally, the Brilliant Sceptic can be inclined to be jealous of others, envying other's gifts or successes and, at times, grudging in offering encouragement or praise to colleagues for a job well done. Maybe Jane was jealous of Sheila being the boss. Oftentimes, the jealously of the Brilliant Sceptic clouds their ability to see the value of others' creative ideas.

The Drivers

The Brilliant Sceptic has the *Be Perfect* and the *Be Strong* drivers in equal measure that maintain their way of dealing with the world and with other people.

The *Be Strong* driver helps Brilliant Sceptics manage their underlying anxiety. As they were growing up, they did not experience the gentle reassurances from their parents when they were feeling afraid, and so learned that they needed to *be strong* when facing difficult situations. Often as children, the Brilliant Sceptics were not made to feel OK when they were emotional. Consequently, they

Don't Talk to the Wall!

learned to hide their real emotions and only show those feelings that were acceptable. The principal emotion that seemed to be permitted was anger, and so the Brilliant Sceptic will have little difficulty in expressing their anger albeit at times in the form of a cold rage. However, this anger masks the more authentic feelings of fear that in their childhood were not acknowledged by their parents.

The *Be Perfect* driver, although to some extent a burden to bear, keeps the Brilliant Sceptic safe from the fear of uncertainty. If they can have everything perfectly done, they don't have to fear the criticism of others or the feelings of anxiety when things don't work out as planned. Their fear of criticism and shame keeps them constantly vigilant to avoid creating situations where they can be found wanting.

Contaminations

The sorts of contaminations that seem to affect the Adult ego state of the Brilliant Sceptic are messages that the child picked up early in life and lodged in their Parent ego state (see Chapter 3). As the Brilliant Sceptic goes through life, they hear such parental voices as: 'Be careful!' 'Don't trust anyone!' 'You never know what's around the corner!' 'Don't fail!' 'Do things properly!' and so on. Such parental messages affect the capacity of the Adult of the Brilliant Sceptics to take risks, to allow themselves to make mistakes, and to be more relaxed with life.

They will often be suspicious and are usually hyper vigilant, and want to be in control. They feel that they need to protect themselves from others.

The contamination from the Child ego state fills the

The Brilliant Sceptic

Brilliant Sceptic with fear and anxiety. Such thoughts as: 'I won't be able to cope!'; 'It's not fair that I have to do everything!'; 'People won't cooperate!'; 'I'm afraid!'; 'I don't trust them!' keep the Brilliant Sceptic on edge, agitated and often rigid in their way of responding to changing situations.

In another sense, we could also say that the Brilliant Sceptic excludes the Child ego state preventing the creative and playful side of the Brilliant Sceptic to grow. It can often look as if the Child has been banished or excluded to prevent the Adult from tapping into the Child energy. This aspect of the Brilliant Sceptic, we show in Fig. 7 where we see the Adult contaminated by the Parent ego state while the Child ego state is excluded. The fact that the Child ego state is excluded means that the Brilliant Sceptic has not got ready access to the playful side of his personality.

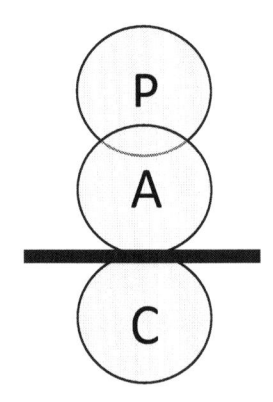

Fig. 7 Exclusion of the Child Ego State and Parent contamination of the adult
(based on Joines & Stewart, 2002)

The Doors of Communication

The open door of the Brilliant Sceptic reveals their thinking. Because they are indeed brilliant in the way they can use their minds in solving complicated scenarios, the way to engage with the Brilliant Sceptic is through their thinking. This is best done by active listening, allowing the Brilliant Sceptic to lay out their thoughts in their logical way. By approaching them through their thinking, we enter into *their* world, and, once we have engaged their thinking, we can then begin to move towards their target door.

The target door of the Brilliant Sceptic opens to their feelings. The Brilliant Sceptic often holds their feelings in check because of the *Be Strong* driver, and will only begin to open the door of their feelings when they have exhausted their thinking on a specific topic. So, in conversation with the Brilliant Sceptic, we reach their emotional life through their thinking! It's only when they have thought clearly that they themselves can feel safe enough to access their emotions.

They need time to get close to people and this happens as they begin to share their thinking with someone who listens and does not criticise or humiliate them as may have happened when they were children.

The trapdoor of the Brilliant Sceptic defends against people criticising their behaviour. The behaviours of the Brilliant Sceptic are different from the behaviours of the Creative Dreamer. Whereas the Creative Daydreamers behaviours were characterised by withdrawal and passivity, the behaviours of the Brilliant Sceptic are more about attack, and being critical, picking holes in others' arguments as a way of keeping their distance from people.

Because of the paranoid nature of the Brilliant Sceptic, they can be critical of others, ready to confront and at times rather aggressive because of their need to be in control so as to stay safe.

When communicating with the Brilliant Sceptic, we may want to challenge their way of behaving. We may have been hurt by what they said or did. However, if we approach the Brilliant Sceptic with a view to changing their behaviour, we will certainly fail. We need to remember that it is only through their open door (thinking) that we can make the initial contact. Then we approach their target door (feelings). When both those doors have been opened, we do not need to do anything further.

By making contact through the first two doors, the Brilliant Sceptic will automatically begin to modify their behaviour, leaving aside the fear that causes them to attack the source of their discomfort. When their thinking and feelings are connected, then they do not feel the need to defend against feelings to protect themselves in the same way.

In the normal dynamics of the Brilliant Sceptic, they move from their strong thinking immediately to their behaviour that is characterised by blame, criticism and cynicism. They skip the feeling dimension. It is only when someone engages with their thinking and then links the thinking with their feeling that their behaviour begins to change.

Beliefs or Statements of the Brilliant Sceptic

1. I like to know all the details of a plan before I agree to it.

2. I find it difficult to believe what people tell me. I think they may be after something.

3. I find it hard to give in when I am arguing because I know I'm right.

4. I get impatient when people don't do what they promise to do.

5. I like to check up on people when I give them a task to do in order to see that they are making progress.

6. Sometimes I find it difficult to delegate tasks to others.

7. I can get angry and frustrated when things don't work out.

8. I sometime find it hard to be sympathetic to people with problems.

9. At times I can be jealous when I see others doing better than I am.

10. I am often more in touch with my anger than with my fear.

11. If you want a job done well, do it yourself.

Count the number of the statements or beliefs that you consider true for you. Total: _____

The Charming Manipulator

CHAPTER SEVEN

The Charming Manipulator

"The game is getting old, and I don't know if it's because I've mastered the art of it, or if I just have some weird attention-deficit-disorder when it comes to getting my way all the time, every time."
Kris Kidd

Joanne was a real schemer. It wasn't that she was telling lies, but she seemed to be able to bend the truth beyond recognition. And she always got what she wanted even though it appeared that she was simply helping out. Before you knew it, she was away on another trip – this time to Vietnam - with the excuse that it would benefit the organisation.

People were afraid to challenge her even though Joanne herself seemed to confront everyone if she didn't feel they should get what they asked for. She would launch an attack out of the blue if things didn't go according to her plans, and could storm out of a meeting, leaving the rest of the group nonplussed. Then, the next day she would carry on as if nothing happened. She could turn on the charm at will, and then turn it off equally quickly.

Generally speaking, Joanne was quite engaging, and the life and soul of the party. She had a story for every situation, and often entertained her colleagues with jokes and wisecracks. She would keep her group in stitches with stories that sounded convincing, but which often came more from her imagination than from reality.

At times she made some serious mistakes, and yet she always managed to wriggle out of the situation, often implicating others in something they had nothing to do with. Suddenly they found themselves under attack when the real culprit was Joanne. Or they found themselves undertaking jobs that really Joanne should have done. How did she do it? She seemed to be able to turn the tables on any situation where she came out best, leaving others to pick up the pieces.

The Clinical Picture

Charming Manipulators (or the antisocial personality) combine the engaging and attractive feature of charm with a rather subversive side to their character that they use in order to get what they want by hook or by crook. They like to draw attention to themselves.

As children, Charming Manipulators learned to be manipulative for good reasons. Some may have experienced their parents as absent most of the time. Others may have experienced their parents as lovingly attentive, overly attentive at times, anticipating their every need, and giving them everything they wanted. With time, however, these same parents grew weary of the effort required to respond to the growing needs of their children. Sometimes they rather abruptly stopped being the attentive parents they had been, and became instead somewhat neglectful at least in the eyes of their children. It may have been that the parents recognised that they needed to pull back from being overly caring, and set limits to what they did for their child, but to their child it appeared that they were abandoning him or her. A fear of abandonment features large in the experience of the Charming Manipulator as well as a fear of being smothered, trapped or controlled.

Children react with some concern and panic to this withdrawal of privileges, and begin to work out strategies to obtain what they want. They feel they will *never* get what they wish for simply by asking directly. Strategies such as temper tantrums, sulking or expressions of anger consequently go to make up their repertoire of stratagems to get what they need. Eventually, children hit upon the ideal formula of charm that seems to achieve everything they want. So, instead of asking directly for what they require, Charming Manipulators work out ways of achieving this aim without having to experience a refusal. Joanne was a perfect example of this.

Recognizing Charming Manipulators

As Charming Manipulators move into adulthood, they sharpen their skills in manipulating people and situations in order to get what they feel entitled to. Sometimes such strategies may develop into illegal activities that end up with the person in prison. Others end up as entrepreneurs, politicians and lawyers. However, for others again, manipulation simply becomes a way of interacting with people so as to obtain what Charming

Manipulators feel they have a right to.

At the basis of a Charming Manipulator's way of acting is the belief that they will not get what they want by asking directly. They may even have the belief that they will *never* get what they want if they are honest about their needs. So, they develop sophisticated techniques to achieve their aims and obtain their desires.

The Charming Manipulator may have a low frustration tolerance when they don't get what they want, and when they feel they are not succeeding by charm, they can become rather nasty and vindictive. They can be single-minded and rather careless in the way they treat others, and they can also be inclined to view other people as simply a means to get what they feel they need.

Frequently, Charming Manipulators also feel the need for excitement and drama. They get bored with routine, and seek ways and means to make life more like an adventure. They love starting things, but then quickly lose interest in the project, and want to move on to something more stimulating. They enjoy having a high profile and quickly abandon anything that does not give them the attention they need.

At times, Charming Manipulators can also be highly irresponsible, willing to cross the line to grab what they want irrespective of moral issues. In a sense, they seem to work more with their Child ego state, and appear to have banished any trace of a Parent ego state that would point out their selfish behaviour.

Whereas the portrait of Charming Manipulators does not appear pleasant, they can be great to have around as they bring life and energy to a group. It is also important to realise that this adaptation grew out of the panic of the child who felt that their feelings or needs were not being responded to, and therefore they were forced to submerge any feelings of weakness or gentleness in order to survive in what they considered a somewhat neglectful or unloving environment. There are various degrees in the expression of the Charming Manipulator, going from mild mild-flirting and charming activities that can be amusing to notice, to criminal acts that unfortunately leave other people hurt and exploited.

The Drivers

The Charming Manipulator is driven by the compulsion to *Be Strong* and *Please Others.* This combination of drivers goes to develop an ability to manage feelings of hurt and disappointment and to engage others in acceding to their demands.

The *Be Strong* driver contributes to the suppression of feelings of compassion, kindness, gentleness and many of the more humane feelings. By suppressing these feelings for people, Charming Manipulators are able to pursue their own agenda or outwit you with their clever thinking. This driver allows them not to be overly concerned for others, or at least to put their own needs and wants before other people.

It is also true that the *Be Strong* driver goes to suppress the feelings of hurt, disappointment and anxiety that the Charming Manipulators must have felt when their parents were no longer meeting their needs. It was as if the trauma of feeling abandoned or neglected had to be deadened in order for the person to begin to plan how best to get their needs met.

The *Please Others* driver is often used to charm the

pants off people, but for ulterior motives – that is, to get something from them. In many ways, this driver could be better labelled as a *Please Me* driver, because most of the energy of the Charming Manipulator is directed to scheming or more kindly towards strategizing in order to get what he or she wants. Sometimes, in their work they may do great good for others once they get the attention that they need. Often they may head up large charity appeals that have a high profile aspect to them, and which bring them great fame and popularity, as well as helping the poor and underprivileged.

This combination of *Please Others* and *Be Strong* thus provide Charming Manipulators with the necessary ammunition to make their way through life, ensuring that they get what they want by whatever means they think necessary.

As a child, Charming Manipulators discovered that they would be OK in the eyes of their parents when they were charming and pleasant. They could get what they wanted if they put on an act that made their parents smile or laugh. They also discovered that if they hid their real feelings of hurt and disappointment, they could work out ways to get what they needed. If they didn't get it by fair means, there were always the foul means!

Contaminations

Usually, people use their three ego states in the course of their day. The Parent ego state holds the opinions, prejudices of the person's own parents. But the Parent ego state also holds the ethical values that the parent had and which they passed on to their children. In a sense, the Parent ego state offers the Adult an ethical code to inform

Don't Talk to the Wall!

the Adult with regard to the choices people in their Adult ego state make.

Charming Manipulators are inclined to engage in a process that excludes the Parent ego state. This process of exclusion can be diagrammed as we see in Fig. 8.

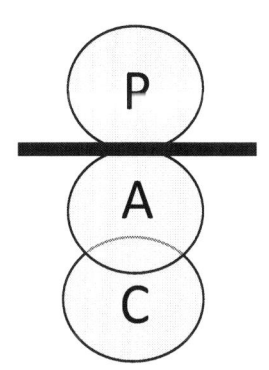

Fig. 8 Exclusion of the Parent ego state with Contamination of the Adult by the Child ego state (based on Joines and Stewart, 2002)

Charming Manipulators ignore or block the Parent ego state so that the Child ego state can be free from any constrictions from the moral voice of the parent. The Adult ego state therefore works in collaboration with the Child ego state to work out clever plans to achieve what the Child ego state wants. The Adult ego state thus becomes contaminated by the Child ego state so that the voice of the Child ego state predominates.

With the Charming Manipulator, we have both exclusion and a contamination. In a sense, the Adult is contaminated by the absence of the Parent, or to put it another way, the Adult and Child cooperate to help the Child get what he or she wants, and the Parent is silenced so as not to interfere with the demands of the Child ego state.

The Doors of Communication

Communicating with Charming Manipulators is a rather tricky process. The main reason for this is that the trapdoor of the Charming Manipulator is their thinking faculty. So, in communicating with them, it is almost impossible to succeed by using a rational approach. They are masters of evasion, and no logical arguments will work to overcome their innate capacity to wriggle out of any situation. You can offer the most logical arguments to the Charming Manipulator, but they will bamboozle you with complicated reasoning that will leave you powerless, confused and frustrated. We have to approach them through their open door, which is the door of behaviour.

The behaviour of the Charming Manipulator is manipulation and therefore, they need to be caught manipulating. By catching them out, the Charming Manipulator will enjoy the game of cat and mouse. They know that they are clever, and admire people who are equally clever. So, with the Charming Manipulator, we need to catch them at their own game. This is the entry point to reaching their target door.

The target door of Charming Manipulators by a process of elimination has to be the feeling door. At the heart of Charming Manipulators are the feelings that drive them to manipulate. Often a combination of feelings such as disappointment, desire, excitement, hurt can come together to motivate the Charming Manipulator to work out schemes to get what they feel they need. In communicating with them, therefore, we firstly challenge their manipulation in a playful way, and then empathically seek to uncover their real feelings.

I use the word empathically, because we could

become rather persecutory and parental as we catch them out in their manipulation. Should we approach them in this critical manner we will only succeed in forcing them into even more clever strategies of dissimulation and deceit. We need to get behind the external behaviour of manipulation to understand the emotions of Charming Manipulators who may be feeling misunderstood and disappointed that their needs are not being met. By targeting the feeling door, we can begin to understand the Charming Manipulator and they, in turn, can begin to think more clearly as to how to get what they want in an open and honest way.

Beliefs or Statements of the Charming Manipulator

1. I often feel I'll never get what I want.
2. If I can't get what I want by asking directly, I'll work out ways to get it without asking.
3. I like being clever at planning projects and proposals
4. I often find people difficult and unwilling to go along with my ideas.
5. I like being popular and seen by others as pleasant and enthusiastic.
6. I don't like having to go into detail about my plans.
7. When people don't go along with me I get angry and, at times, rather vindictive.
8. I am good at seeing the big picture and imagining what the future will look like.
9. I easily get bored with routine.
10. Sometimes I'm not honest with regard to how I get money - bending the law is not the same as breaking it.
11. I like being the centre of attention

Count the number of the statements or beliefs that you consider true for you. Total: _____

The Responsible Workaholic

CHAPTER EIGHT

The Responsible Workaholic

"I missed my dad a lot growing up, even though we were together as a family. My dad was really a workaholic."
Steven Spielberg

Monsignor Roberto was an amazing man. He arrived at the parish office at 7.00 a.m. each morning, having spent time in prayer before that. From seven until eight-thirty he dealt with correspondence and emails, and then went for his breakfast, when he took the time to read the morning papers.

His daily 10 o'clock mass was well attended because each day he prepared a homily on the readings for the liturgy, and people found he was always interesting and inspiring in what he had to say. Monsignor Roberto took the task of delivering his homily seriously. He would spend time each evening thinking a lot about what he would preach about, often looking up interesting quotations from the latest books on spirituality.

After Mass, he would go to the parish office to find out

from Mary, his secretary, what appointments he had that day. He could have a funeral or a wedding, or a visit to the local primary or secondary school, or that day might have been the day for visiting the sick in hospital.

Many a day he would grab a bite of a sandwich and a cup of tea while en route to his next appointment, or take no lunch at all. In the afternoons, he often went on house visitation to the elderly members of the parish, leaving the evenings free to visit the homes of the younger couples who were at work during the day.

He used to take Wednesdays off each week to get a game of golf with his fellow priest friends, but lately he has had to cancel these outings because of the pressure to fit everything in.

Recently, however, Monsignor Roberto has begun to get headaches, and finds that his sleep is being disrupted. He knows he should take it easy, but when he does take a day off, he feels guilty that he is not getting everything done.

The parishioners love Monsignor Roberto, as he is always available when they need him. Of late, however, they notice that he can be rather touchy at times, and reacts quite defensively when they make any suggestions about the running of the parish.

The Clinical Picture

Responsible Workaholics are exactly that; they are highly responsible and are able to maintain an incredible workload. People are always amazed at the amount of tasks they can achieve in the course of any one day, and even when they are busy, they willingly take on more jobs if requested to do so.

The Responsible Workaholic

When Responsible Workaholics are asked how their day was, they will invariably talk about the amount of work they covered. Seldom will they talk about their feelings or about their social engagements. For them life and work are almost synonymous. In fact, they will often introduce themselves by giving their title as in, "Hello, I'm David and I'm an architect.'

People depend on Responsible Workaholics because they are so dependable and honest. You get what you see. They don't create a fuss, but simply get down to the job and do it very well. Perfection is their virtue and their burden. They are never satisfied with a job half-done, and will persevere without rest until the task is completed. Often they, like Monsignor Roberto, will go without eating because they get caught up in getting the job finished.

Frequently they will postpone a pleasurable activity until they have fulfilled their responsibilities. So, birthdays, holiday breaks, going to the cinema are often put off because they get caught up in finishing off a job. Then they never manage to actually celebrate the birthday or go on the holiday because some other job or duty has to be undertaken. Or if they do go, they are constantly worrying about the work piling up, and may cut a visit, holiday or treat short in order to get back to the work.

Recognizing Responsible Workaholics

One of the features of the Responsible Workaholic is that they almost never celebrate the successful conclusion of a task. Instead, they are a bit like the hill walker who reaches the apparent summit of a mountain only to discover that there is another hill that needs to be climbed before the final summit is reached.

Responsible Workaholics also find criticism difficult to take. Any negative remarks feed into their anxiety that they might make a mistake. When they hear the slightest hint of a negative remark, they will seek either to justify what they have done, or increase their effort to avoid any possibility of blame. This inability to take criticism plays into their perfectionist streak that cannot bear any trace of fault or imperfection.

They can also be tense and even physically hold themselves rigidly, walking in a measured or controlled way. Often they can suffer from aches and pains as a result of their unbending posture. They can also suffer from headaches due to the tense way they keep worrying about what they have yet to do. Sometimes their sleep patterns are affected when they continue to worry about the work they have to accomplish the following day.

They speak clearly making sure that they do not omit any detail from what they want to say. But in the detail, they often lose the passion and enthusiasm for their subject. In the fear of being found out that they do not know everything, they will qualify each statement they make until the number of parenthesis can leave the listener lost in a maze of sub-clauses.

Responsible Workaholics can become obsessive about their diet and their environment. They examine the contents of the food packages they buy, and can have theories about health that lead them to assume strange eating habits. And they can also become obsessive about the order and cleanliness of their surroundings, spending much time in tidying and cleaning. They will love to have their books in alphabetical order on their bookshelves, and like ticking off their to-do list on a regular basis.

The Drivers

The principal driver of the Responsible Workaholics is the *Be Perfect* driver. In some cases, the *Be Perfect* is often accompanied by the *Be Strong* driver because Responsible Workaholics may also have a Creative Daydreamer surviving adaptation (see Chapter 5).

Responsible Workaholics develop in family situations where the parents are severely critical of their children, or may have been too strong in encouraging them to overachieve. They may have been given a lot of praise for *doing* but little praise for *being.* It's as if the parents send an unconscious injunction *Don't Be a Child* to their baby. They cannot cope with the growing infant, and from an early age attempt to make them responsible far too prematurely. This demand for achievement can be loaded onto the first born especially when the next child appears. Then the eldest is given responsibilities that only adults should have to assume.

The critical voice of the parent can sometimes express the parents' unconscious wish that their child had not been born! It may be that they expected a boy and a girl arrived or *vice versa.* So, the Little Professor of the child (the early Adult in the child) makes a decision that in order to continue to exist, they will become perfect. By being perfect, they believe they will earn the love and acceptance of the parents and be OK.

As the critical voice of the Controlling or Critical Parent becomes introjected or incorporated into the growing child, and then through adolescence and adulthood, the inner critic is born. No longer does the person need the nagging voice of the criticising parent, because they have swallowed the these aspects within themselves, and begun to act in response to this inner persecutor! Thus, the Child ego state feels compelled to be perfect in order to get the internal Critical Parent off their case.

At the same time that the *Be Perfect* driver evolves, the *Be Strong* driver may develop in tandem in response to the unconscious negative messages or injunctions from the parents and as a result of the Responsible Workaholic developing some schizoid characteristics. Messages such as *Don't Feel, Don't Be Close, Don't Be a Child* prevent children from expressing the full range of emotional responses in relation to their experience. Eventually, children realize that it is safer not to express any authentic feelings and avoid the critical voices of their parents. This ban on expressing feelings leads Responsible Workaholics to discount feelings and consider them more of a nuisance than an important indicator of their connection with others and with the world.

Contaminations

The principal source of contamination with the Responsible Workaholic comes from the Parent ego state (Fig. 9). As mentioned above, the main cause of the compulsion towards perfection arises from the Critical Parent or what is also known as the Controlling Parent (Chapter 3). The energy that resides in the Adult is diminished by the presence of negative Parent energy that dilutes the capacity of the Adult to feel an unconditional OKness, and leads them to work themselves to the bone.

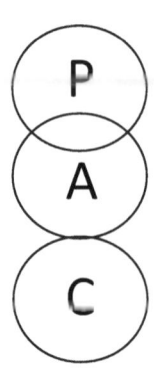

Fig. 9 Contamination of the Adult by the Parent Ego State
(Berne, 1961)

Responsible Workaholics can, in their unguarded moments, show real anger and frustration when things are not working out. Anger, at the same time, is a problem for them because they view anger as a fault, and therefore can be inclined to beat themselves up when they display it. What they are not often in touch with is sadness, the sadness of loss. They need to grieve their lost childhood, when they had to grow up too quickly, and assume responsibility at an early age. They also need to grieve the fact that they were not loved unconditionally, but had to perform to gain any form of approval. As they reflect on their past, they may eventually be able to get in touch with their justifiable anger and resentment. The hope is that with time, they will then be able to experience sadness and grief as they come to a level of forgiveness for parents who did not give them what they needed and deserved.

The Doors of Communication

Just like the Brilliant Sceptic, the trapdoor of the Responsible Workaholic is behaviour. But the behaviour of the Responsible Workaholic is slightly different from that of the Brilliant Sceptic. While the Brilliant Sceptic is inclined to blame and criticize others, the Responsible Workaholic is probably more likely to blame themselves. They are their own worst enemy. The behaviour of the Responsible Workaholic is along perfectionist lines and borders on the obsessive behaviour. They continue to focus on getting things right and achieving more and more.

We may want to change that behaviour, but here again we are doomed to failure since we are dealing with their trapdoor. And, of course, if they are battling against a message from their early childhood that they should not exist (by working without a break to ensure their existence) then it would be foolhardy to get them to stop working. Work is what is keeping them alive.

So, the open door to the Responsible Workaholic is through their thinking. By engaging with their thoughts and ideas, we make a good connection. The Responsible Workaholic is a clear and intelligent thinker without any fuzziness or ulterior messages. They say it as it is, albeit with lots of clauses and subclauses.

When, however, their thinking becomes obsessive, then they are no longer in their lucid and free state, and their behaviour follows the persecutory voice of their Parent voice. What happens with them is that they move directly from their thoughts to action without engaging their feelings. This is especially true with the obsessive thoughts. They go from thoughts to action without giving real attention to their feelings of scare that lie at the basis of obsession.

When we want therefore to engage with them, we

begin as we said above with their thoughts, and then move to their feelings. Once we make this emotional connection, we do not have to worry with their behaviours. Gradually, they will open their trapdoor and begin to soften the inner critical voice, and give themselves permission to relax and take time off for themselves.

What is helpful to remember is that in dealing with the Responsible Workaholic they respond well to requests. Whereas the Creative Daydreamer needs a more directive approach, the Responsible Workaholic works more from an Adult-to-Adult process. By asking for exactly what we want, the Responsible Workaholic will more than likely respond positively, even when, at times, it might also be important for them to decline our requests. Hence, we need to be careful not to overload the Responsible Workaholic by asking too much of them.

Beliefs or Statements of the Responsible Workaholic

1. I never have enough time to do all the things I have to do.

2. I like making lists of the jobs I have to do, and then ticking them off as they are completed.

3. Sometimes I feel I am taken for granted.

4. I prefer to get a job finished rather than take a break in the middle of doing it.

5. I like to keep my personal space neat and tidy.

6. Even when I'm feeling tired or hungry, I prefer to keep going.

7. I can often feel angry but I seldom feel sad.

8. When I treat myself to some luxury, I can often feel guilty.

9. I take criticism personally.

10. I hardly ever allow myself to cry.

11. I don't like being wrong and will attempt to justify any apparent mistake.

Count the number of the statements or beliefs that you consider true for you. Total: _____

The Enthusiastic Over-Reactor

CHAPTER NINE

The Enthusiastic Over-Reactor

*"Pain is real when you get other people to believe in it.
If no one believes in it but you,
your pain is madness or hysteria."*
Naomi Wolf

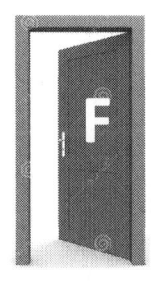

Catherine is like phosphorous on water! She has boundless energy and seems never to tire. She can stay up all hours preparing visual aids for some presentation she is giving, or can spend hours on end writing to various friends with whom she regularly corresponds.

Everything for her is 'marvellous' or 'wonderful' and people are 'fabulous' and 'fantastic'. She continually affirms everyone she meets, wanting to see only their good points and delights in the successes of others.

You can hear her screeches and laughter a mile away as she rushes around the house to meet everyone and have a chat. She hardly draws a breath when she is telling a story of an adventure she had, or of a party she attended. Her smiles and laughs punctuate her stories as she seeks to communicate her love for life.

She is always doing jobs for other people, even when they are quite happy to do the jobs themselves. She can be inclined to 'smother' people, offering them all sorts of favours and presents. This is when she is in a good mood.

While Catherine loves parties and outings, frequently she seems to go into some sort of 'low' after the event. It's as if she enjoys the moment, and then finds the after effect somewhat depressing.

When things do not go well for her, Catherine can get upset, spending long hours telling of her woes and of the injustices that she feels she has suffered. Her tears and anger can lead her to react with vindictiveness towards the object of her frustration. When she is upset, the whole house has to suffer her tantrums, and no arguments will smooth the ruffled waters.

And so, Catherine can be loving and delightful when things go well, and then can become uncontrollable when she is hurt or wronged. Her highs and lows are obvious, and many people like the honesty she shows in reaction to people and events. You definitely know where you stand with Catherine. While it is obvious how Catherine is feeling at any time, sometimes people find it difficult to live with her, as they never know when she is going to be up or down. This uncertainty can mean that people are metaphorically walking on eggshells for fear of upsetting her.

The Clinical Picture

The Enthusiastic Over-Reactor is also classified as the histrionic or hysterical personality. It is often the case that the Enthusiastic Over-Reactors have come from families where the parents treated them as children long after they had left their childhood. It is almost as if the parents did not want their child to grow up. This can be the case when the child is either an only child, or the last in a line of children where the parents want the last born to stay eternally young. Allied to this desire to foster the Peter Pan effect, the parents of the Enthusiastic Over-Reactor can discourage their child from thinking, and instead encourage them to feel. Thus, the child grows to adulthood with the belief that they cannot think that clearly, and that feelings are more important anyway. It can also be that their parents gave lots of strokes for *being* but not for *doing*. As a result, they lack confirmation of their competence.

Recognizing Enthusiastic Over-Reactors

Enthusiastic Over-Reactors are characterized by a high level of excitability as we saw in the description of Catherine. This excitability is in reaction to people and events that impact on them. In fact, what we are talking about is the *over-reaction* to things that happen to this type of personality. Their responses are exaggerated and dramatic, far in excess of the reaction of the other personality adaptations to people or situations.

At an unconscious level, the Enthusiastic Over-Reactor seeks to be the centre of attention. They may have been the favourite son or daughter of their mother or father, and found that when they were not getting sufficient attention, they simply upped the ante until they got the reaction they wanted. So, temper tantrums, crying bouts and sulking became the tools they employed to get a reaction from their parents. Alternatively, they become seductive, metaphorically fluttering their eyelashes to

The Enthusiastic Over-Reactor

draw the other person into their world. In many ways, they find it difficult to separate facts from feelings; when they feel sad they believe that the situation is intrinsically a sad one even when others may have different reactions to the same event.

They come across as rather immature and self-centred, appearing to be more like children than adults. In many ways, they behave as if they are needy, and indeed they often carry on in a manner that shows a high level of dependence.

The Drivers

The two main drivers of the Enthusiastic Over-Reactor are the *Please Me/Others* and the will often have the *Hurry Up* driver as an auxiliary driver.

The *Please Me/Others* driver either involves a compulsion to get the other person to love, care, and pay attention to them, or alternatively it involves trying incessantly to give love, care and attention to others. In either case, the focus is on the Enthusiastic Over-Reactor and the flow of emotion is towards them. In their childhood, they discovered that their parents reacted positively to them when they went out of their way to please the parents, or when they seductively sought to be caressed by the parents. The flow of emotion was what kept the relationships going, and the greater the emotional charge, the more alive the child felt.

Consequently, the Enthusiastic Over-Reactor feels alive only when there is a significant flow of emotional reactions. So, Catherine as described above feels alive when she is feeling, whereas she finds thinking draining and challenging. When she was a child she got no recognition for her intelligence, but was stroked when she came across as 'cute'.

The *Hurry Up* driver further characterizes the Enthusiastic Over-Reactors' upbringing. It seems as if they were OK once they went about things smartly. Often the Enthusiastic Over-Reactors' parents modelled this frenetic activity, and created an atmosphere in the house where everything had to be done quickly if not efficiently. In many cases, things were not done adequately simply due to the fact that they were rushed. Now as an adult, the Enthusiastic Over-Reactor is inclined to focus on getting the job completed in the shortest possible time, and thereby making many mistakes and omitting important details. It sometimes appears that the Enthusiastic Over-Reactor wants to finish quickly in order to please the Parent figure and to get praise for completing a job ahead of time.

Contaminations

The main contamination of the Enthusiastic Over-Reactor comes from the Child ego state (Fig. 10). The

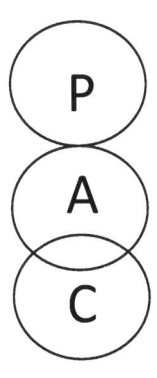

Fig. 10 Contamination of the Adult by the Child Ego State
(Berne, 1961)

Adult, therefore, is often compromised by the feeling that the Enthusiastic Over-Reactor has never grown up. Childish fears, anxieties, uncertainties can predominate.

Enthusiastic Over-Reactors can feel child-like emotions of enthusiasm, happiness that links them directly back to the time when they were children. These emotions can, of course, be part of the Adult, but when we talk about contamination, we are referring to those historical ego states that invade the present reality (Clarkson & Gilbert, 1988:20). Often Enthusiastic Over-Reactors feel as they did when they were in their childhood, and look for parent figures that will offer them the recognition and affection that they so badly needed when growing up.

The Doors of Communication

The Enthusiastic Over-Reactor is unique in having feelings as their open door; none of the other personality adaptations has feelings as the initial point of contact. Often therefore, people find it quite difficult to manage the escalation of feelings that the Enthusiastic Over-Reactors can generate, and the over-reactions that they demonstrate in the face of their difficulties. The mechanism of the Enthusiastic Over-Reactor is that they go directly from strong feelings (their open door) to act out these feelings often in inappropriate behaviours (their trapdoor). So, they move from their open door to their trapdoor without going through the thinking target door.

In order, therefore, to communicate effectively with the Enthusiastic Over-Reactor, the person needs to really listen to the strong feelings being expressed. This becomes difficult when the Enthusiastic Over-Reactor is prone to act out in exaggerated ways while they are feeling. They can become violent, abusive, throwing things around the place, while venting their anger or disappointment. The tendency of the listener is to try to contain the behaviour and to get the person to calm down. This often does not work. Because behaviour is their trapdoor, it is often pointless to attempt to challenge or criticize the behaviour of the Enthusiastic Over-Reactor. When the emphasis is put on changing their behaviour, all that happens is that the feelings continue to be given free reign, and the acting out increases exponentially.

The biggest challenge is to be a nurturing and caring listening ear to the Enthusiastic Over-Reactor. They need to experience the listener as empathic and attuned to *their* feelings. They also need the person to understand *why* they feel so strongly, and to validate their experience so that it is normalised. Unless this approach is taken, the Enthusiastic Over-Reactor will intensify the feelings and may act out in ways that are damaging to themselves or to others.

Much time is needed to connect with the feelings of the Enthusiastic Over-Reactor, and the listener needs to bracket his or her judgement with regard to the reasonableness of the feelings expressed. If this is done, eventually the Enthusiastic Over-Reactor will exhaust themselves and begin to allow the target door (their thinking) to be approached. In fact, it usually does not take long for them to move into thinking once they feel that their feelings are acknowledged.

When the Enthusiastic Over-Reactor allows the target door to be opened, they begin to reflect on their feelings

The Enthusiastic Over-Reactor

and the on the reasons why they feel so strongly. This is an important moment, and it will often be a case of see-sawing back and forth between feeling and thinking until the thinking comes more into focus. Once this happens, the behaviour of the Enthusiastic Over-Reactor becomes more contained, the feelings become more measured, and the storm calms down quite quickly.

Beliefs or Statements of the Enthusiastic Over-Reactor

1. I sometimes feel like I have never grown up.
2. I love excitement and adventure.
3. I can't understand when people are so cold and unemotional.
4. I like to get things done quickly.
5. I feel hurt when people don't recognise me when I achieve something great.
6. I sometimes regret when I said or did something hurtful to others.
7. I often find that people don't really understand me.
8. When I have a friend I want to really connect with them but sometimes find that they back off.
9. I often feel disappointed and annoyed when people don't return my calls.
10. I often feel sad and lonely.
11. I often seem to feel afraid of the future when other people seem to take it in their stride.

Count the number of the statements or beliefs that you consider true for you. Total: _____

The Playful Resister

CHAPTER TEN

The Playful Resister

"I thought of the things that had happened to me over the years, and of how little I had made happen."
Julian Barnes

Richard finds life a struggle. He is bright and knowledgeable, but somehow he doesn't ever realize his full potential. It seems that he often begins a task, but never fully finishes what he starts. Even when he does complete a job, there is always something wrong with the end product. Recently, he negotiated the sale of an important property, but mixed up the papers for the final deal, and found that his boss took the client away from him and did the job himself. In his previous employment as one of the graphic designers for a magazine, he would find himself constantly hounded by his supervisor to deliver the goods on time. Eventually he left because he felt she was bullying him. Just because he happened to be a few days late with final copy! He felt life was unfair.

Richard sometimes finds it difficult to fully grasp what people want of him. The other day he was asked to draw up a marketing plan for one of the prestigious office blocks in the city. This wasn't a problem for him, but he thought he would do it more creatively rather than just submit the usual stereotypical plan. When he presented the final draft to his boss, the reaction was awful. His boss shouted at him, telling him to go back and do the thing again, and this time according to the normal protocols. All he was trying to do was to present the plan in an exciting way, and now he was being attacked for taking some initiative. People just did not understand. He thinks he won't stay with the company much longer. If they don't recognize his skills, he can get another job. They are not a nice group of people. They seem to be only concerned with making money, whereas he sees there is more to life than that. He's damned if he is going to cooperate with that attitude that puts money before people. At the same time he realizes that he has to bring home money for Mary and the three kids. Why does everything need to be a struggle?

The Clinical Picture

Playful Resisters in the more classical literature are called passive aggressives. They express their anger in a passive way, by sabotaging anything they touch. They also cause other people to become angry and aggressive in reaction to their passivity.

Playful Resisters developed this behaviour in response to perceived over-control on the part of their parents. As they were growing up, they experienced their parents as too strong, too demanding, and they felt trapped by this domination. However, rather than engaging in open battle with people more powerful than themselves, they discovered that they could thwart and frustrate their parents by being passive. Richard is a good example of such an approach to life. The resistance of Playful Resisters is an unconscious process, but eventually they become experts in countering the parents' control. As Playful Resisters move from childhood into adolescence, they often feel a mounting resentment towards their overly controlling parents. In reaction, they come to a decision that no one will make them do anything if they don't want to do it. Much of this reasoning takes place out of full awareness.

Recognizing Playful Resisters

Often Playful Resisters will fume inside at the demands of others, and they will actively and stubbornly refuse to cooperate with those they perceive are too oppressive. Whereas they are cooperative with those they like, they simply withdraw from those they find difficult, or even deliberately go against them for the sake of maintaining their own autonomy. However, in so doing they often sabotage themselves and their potential for growth and development. Their determination that 'nobody is going to control me' puts them in a position where they unconsciously miss the opportunities for advancement. Their passive behaviour can also, at times, find expression in overt violence. Violence is a passive behaviour because ultimately it does not achieve what it hoped for in the first place (Schiff, 1975: 10-14). The Playful Resister's violence similarly only succeeds in creating situations where there is an on-going battle between two opposing forces that refuse to capitulate.

Frequently, Playful Resisters demonstrate their resistance to change by forgetfulness, thoughtless mistakes and general lack of attention to detail.

The Drivers

The drivers associated with the Playful Resisters are the *Try Hard* with the *Be Strong* driver in an auxiliary position.

The *Try Hard* is unique to the Playful Resister. This is the classical response they make when confronted with an over-controlling Critical Parent. Playful Resisters will *try hard*. They will supposedly put a lot of effort into what they are doing, but never actually manage to achieve or complete what they set out to do. It seems that they learned that once they *tried hard* their parents were satisfied. They go though life *trying hard* but never succeeding. For the Playful Resister, the important thing is to struggle, to put effort into something even though the outcome will not yield a good result. Everything for them is a struggle. One of the clearest indicators of the *Try Hard* is the practice of procrastination where plans are shelved and tasks left undone. In addition to the procrastination, what is often more obvious are the seemingly unconscious sabotages that the Playful Resister can employ. They often will create major problems for others by failing to finish jobs assigned to them or by 'inadvertently' ruining a project.

The derivation of the word sabotage goes back to the industrial revolution when the workers in Holland would throw their wooden clogs (*sabots* in French) into the machinery to stop the conveyor belts running, and thus give themselves a break. Hence the word '*sabot*age'!

The *Be Strong* driver allows the Playful Resister to hide their real feelings from others. They secretly conceal their seething anger and resentment so as to use this energy to resist any form of control. They also want to hide their dependence on others, and the *Be Strong* driver allows them to camouflage their real feelings.

Contaminations

Playful Resisters have a double contamination that paralyses the power of the Adult to function to its fullest potential. We see this graphically in Fig. 11.

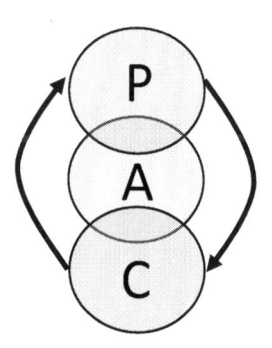

Fig. 11 The Parent-Child Impasse
(based on Joines & Stewart, 2002)

Here we have an internal battle between two great powers. The Parent ego state sends messages to the Child ego state. Such messages could be commands like, 'Do, what you're told!' or 'Hurry up, and get this done!' All the commands are directive. While this may work for the Creative Daydreamer, all it creates in the Child of the Playful Resister is resistance. So, in response to the Parent commands, the Playful Resister's response is a resounding

The Playful Resister

'No, I won't!'. This creates an impasse where both parties are stuck and neither can resolve the situation unless one of the parties changes position.

The Doors of Communication

The open door of the Playful Resister is linked to their behaviour. However, unlike the Creative Daydreamer who also has behaviour as the open door, the behaviour of the Playful Resister is resistance through passivity. The Creative Daydreamer's behaviour is withdrawal. In fact, we could say that Playful Resisters also withdraw but in their case they do so in a more oppositional way. They resist. Therefore, the way to connect with them needs to acknowledge this resistance and avoid getting into a battle of wills. Simply attempting to overcome their resistance will not work, and will only lead to greater resistance. Playful Resisters cannot be beaten.

You will also notice that the door sequence of the Playful Resister is identical to that of the Charming Manipulator – Behaviour, Feeling and Thinking. But here again, the description of the behaviour is different. For the Charming Manipulator, the behaviour is manipulative when they are scheming to get what they want. It is an active and energetic behaviour. For the Playful Resister, as we said, it is passive and resistant. In both cases, however, the trapdoor of thinking involves ways of thinking that are confused, illogical and contradictory.

Consequently, the best approach to Playful Resisters is by being playful. We simply let them know that we recognise their resistance and that we stroke their cleverness at beating the system. By being playful and empathic we connect with their Child ego state, and instead of shifting into the Controlling Parent mode, we move alongside them and join them from a Child ego state.

Having made the connection through the open door, we then move to the target door, which in this case are their feelings. By inviting the Playful Resisters to connect with their feelings, we get to the core of their difficulty – their vengeful anger at being controlled or forced to comply. Once we acknowledge the normality of such a reaction to over-control, and offer the Playful Resister our warm and affirming response, they can let go of their resistance and begin to cooperate in a more responsible way.

For the Playful Resisters, their trapdoor is thinking. Therefore, no amount of reasoning, arguing, confronting or explaining will make the slightest difference with the Playful Resister. They simply resist any form of rational argumentation. Their thinking becomes fuzzy, confused and rigid in the face of opposition or challenge, and they stubbornly hold onto their point of view.

The normal mechanism for Playful Resisters is to move from resistance over to a sort of 'logical' thinking – that is far from logical – that will back up their resistance. Their journey from the open door to the trapdoor skips out the target door of feelings, and because the authentic feelings are missed, the vice-like connection between resistance and skewed thinking cannot be broken. Only when we address their underlying feelings of resentment and rebellious rage with a sympathetic approach will the Playful Resisters begin to cooperate.

Beliefs or Statements of the Playful Resister

1. I am inclined to put things on the long finger (putting off until tomorrow what I need to do today).

2. I often find it difficult to finish the things I set out to do.

3. People can be controlling and domineering.

4. I find it easy to work with people who are kind and understanding.

5. Sometimes I make stupid mistakes when completing a job

6. I find it difficult to express myself clearly enough so that people don't misunderstand what I mean.

7. I am not really satisfied that I am working to my fullest potential.

8. When I am angry I boil inside but seldom do I show it externally.

9. I often come across as calm and relaxed, but inside I am frequently in turmoil.

10. I would like to be more assertive.

11. I sometimes eat and drink too much.

Count the number of the statements or beliefs that you consider true for you. Total: _____

CHAPTER ELEVEN

A View of Time

"Unfortunately, the clock is ticking, the hours are going by.
The past increases, the future recedes.
Possibilities decreasing, regrets mounting."
Haruki Murakami

So, having looked at the various personality types, I hope that you have begun to identify which surviving and which performing adaptations you seem to favour. As mentioned earlier, we have all the adaptations to some extent, but there is probably one surviving adaptation that we use more often than the others, and then we may have one or two performing adaptations. As a further help in identifying which adaptations are most relevant to you, I will present what is known as a 'Process Script'.

Taibi Kahler uses the term 'Process Script' to explain how the personality types play out their Script in the day-to-day life of each individual. He combines the process of the Script with driver behaviour already discussed in Chapter 4 (Kahler, 1978: 205ff; 2008: 103ff; 147ff; 181ff). You can see in Table 2 overleaf how the *drivers* and the Process Script are linked to the various personality types.

Eric Berne devised the idea that our lives are, to a large extent, predetermined by the early decisions we made about how we thought our lives would unfold. In my previous book *Are We Together?* I discuss the idea of Script at length. Suffice it to say here that Script is an

A View of Time

unconscious life plan, based on a decision made in childhood that we seek to live out in the course of our lives (Berne, 1972: 493).

Drivers	Process Script	Personality Types
Be Perfect	Until	Responsible Workaholic
Be Strong	Never	Charming Manipulator
Try Hard	Always	Playful Resister
Please Others	After	Enthusiastic Over-Reactor
Try Hard/ Please Others	Almost 1	Playful Resister
Please Others / Be Perfect	Almost 2	Responsible Workaholic
Be Perfect/ Be Strong	Until/Almost 2	Brilliant Sceptic

Table 2. Drivers, Process Scripts & Personality Types
(Karpman, 1978; Joines & Stewart, 2002 - adapted)

Berne lists the types of Scripts that are connected to time structure as: the *Never*, the *Always*, the *Until*, the *After*, and the *Over and Over* (Almost) Scripts (Berne, 1970:151ff). He links these Scripts with characters in Greek mythology to better portray how the Script works. We will follow his example, referring to the people we have already mentioned in the various personality types, who live out these Process Scripts in their daily lives.

The Never Script

The Greek hero Tantalus was made to stand in a pool of water beneath a fruit tree with low branches, with the fruit ever eluding his grasp, and the water always receding before he could take a drink. He represents the *Never*

Script. So, Tantalus was *never* satisfied, and felt eternally frustrated with life. When he wanted to eat or drink he was *never* able to get what he wanted. It seemed it *never* occurred to him that he could shift his position and get to the water or the fruit!

Both the Charming Manipulator and the Creative Daydreamers often feel that they can *never* get what they want. They often have many wishes and plans, but always feel that they can *never* achieve their deepest desires. Often they blame the situations they find themselves in, thinking that life is cheating them. Like Tantalus, opportunities seem to elude them, and they *never* consider that they can do anything about the situation. So, they can feel frustrated with life and, at the same time, too readily resigned to the fact that the environment is working against them. However, the Charming Manipulator actively works to get what they want despite the belief that underlies their rather devious ways.

The driver *Be Strong* is linked to the *Never* Script because the only way to deal with the belief that the person can *never* get what they want is to dampen all strong feelings of disappointment and accept fate (Kahler, 1975:280ff). Creative Daydreamers have both the *Be Strong* driver and the *Never* Script. They seem to be 'in control' avoiding expressions of anger, sadness and fear, and remaining stoical before a reality that they feel they can *never* change. You remember John who hated parties. He managed to control his feelings of panic and scare by focusing on a picture hanging on the wall and escaping for a cigarette, but he seemed resigned that it would ever be thus (Chapter 5). Charming Manipulators also hide their real feelings of sadness, putting on a brave face in the belief that although they can *never* get they what they want by fair means, they will succeed by manipulation. Joanne, the schemer and Charming Manipulator is a good example of this *Be Strong* driver, where she was able to control her feelings of weakness and scare in order to get her trip to Vietnam by hook or by crook (Chapter 7).

The Always Script

In Greco-Roman mythology, the mortal Arachne was a great weaver who boasted that her skill was greater than that of Athena, goddess of wisdom, weaving and strategy. When Arachne refused to acknowledge that her skill came, in part at least, from the goddess Athena, Athena took offense and set up a contest between the two. Athena saw that Arachne had insulted the gods, and so she ripped Arachne's work into shreds. Arachne hanged herself. Moved to mercy, Athena brought Arachne back to life, but sprinkled her with Hecate's potion, turning her into a spider, and cursing her and her descendants to *always* weave her webs without ever getting a rest.

The *Try Hard* driver is connected to the *Always* Script. We saw Richard feeling under the influence of the *Always* Script (Chapter 10). Whether he is upsetting his boss when he mislays contracts or is late with the graphic design, he seems to feel that nothing will change, and that people are *always* too demanding of him. Like Arachne, he feels condemned to a repeating cycle of frustrated attempts to achieve something worthwhile, but finds himself *always* trapped, and moves on in the hope that the next job will be better. Because, at an unconscious level, Richard believes that things will *always* be the same, his attempts are only attempts, but he never succeeds despite *trying hard*. The *Try Hard* driver seems to be the Playful Resister's only response to what they consider is the inevitable fate that lies before them. Thus the *Try Hard* driver and the *Always* Script go together.

The Until Script

The Greek hero Jason, went in search of the Golden Fleece in order to win back the kingdom for his father. He could not return home *until* he overcame many obstacles in his search for the prized Fleece.

The example of Monsignor Roberto in Chapter 8 exemplifies the *Until* Script. He found he could not take a break *until* he had completed his parish duties, and even forsook his weekly golf outing because he hadn't finished his work. People with the *Until* Script are experts in delayed gratification; and often the delay is quite long, even to the point where the gratification is forgotten!

The *Until* Script is closely linked to the *Be Perfect* driver. Monsignor Roberto appears under the burden of the *Be Perfect* driver. He has a definite timetable, which he observes religiously, and the time he spends working on his homilies points to someone who has an inner critic that keeps him working to the point where he is physically exhausted. He will not take a break *until* he is satisfied that everything is done. So, the Responsible Workaholic is characterised by both the *Be Perfect Driver* and the *Until* Script.

The After Script

In the Greek legend, Damocles used to make comments to the king about his wealth and luxurious life. One day when Damocles complimented the tyrant on his abundance and power, Dionysius turned to Damocles and said, "If you think I'm so lucky, how would you like to try out my life?" Damocles readily agreed, and so Dionysius ordered everything to be prepared for Damocles to experience what life as Dionysius was like. Damocles was enjoying himself immensely until he noticed a sharp sword hovering over his head that was suspended from the ceiling by a strand of horsehair. This, the tyrant explained to Damocles, was what life as a ruler was like. He may have the power and wealth, but afterwards he will pay for it.

The *After Script* refers to the idea that while power and wealth and happiness may appear attractive, afterwards is the realization that none of these three elements is as attractive as they initially appear. The motto of this Script is, according to Berne: 'You can enjoy yourself for a while, but it is *after* that your troubles begin' (Berne, 1970: 151).

This Script applies to Catherine, the phosphorous-on-water lady who sometimes finds that after a party she suffers some sort of party-blues (Chapter 9). She often feels that she will have to pay for the pleasure she had at the party.

The *After* Script can be linked to the *Please Others* driver. The relationship between the two can be explained by the two parts in the statements that the *After Script* often expresses: 'I'm enjoying such and such, but I'll regret...' The person is doing something to please him or herself in the first part of the sentence, and in the second part is the idea that the negative results of the behaviour will somehow displease others. So, in the case of Catherine, the pleasure to the parties is offset by the thought that *afterwards* she will have to catch up with her work, which she failed to complete because of the party.

The Almost (Over and Over) Script

Albert Camus wrote a famous philosophical work on the myth of Sisyphus, the Greek hero (Camus, 2005:115ff). He describes the story thus:

> The gods had condemned Sisyphus to ceaselessly rolling a rock to the top of a mountain, whence the stone would fall back of its own weight. They had thought with some reason that there is no more dreadful punishment than futile and hopeless labour.

Camus goes on to say that the real torture for Sisyphus was that he was conscious of the futility of his efforts. Sisyphus *almost* completes his task, and at the last moment he slips, and the stone rolls back down to the bottom of the hill. So, he has to begin again pushing the stone back up the hill until the weight of it causes him to let it roll back again. He *almost* succeeds.

We saw how Richard was caught up in the *Almost* Script. He *almost* succeeded in selling the house and *almost* succeeded in drawing up the marketing plans for a building block. But in both cases he made significant mistakes leading to his boss becoming frustrated with him (Chapter 10).

The driver *Try Hard* fits well with the *Almost* Script. Instead of succeeding, the person will *Try Hard* and *almost* achieve what he or she wanted to achieve. They will push the stone up the hill, but at the last moment, they will let it fall down again. Frustration and passive aggression characterize this type of Script. By being passive, they also cause considerable frustration and aggression in others. Richard is the prime example.

Taibi Kahler identifies two types of the *Almost* Script (Kahler, 1978:216). The first one we have already described with Sisyphus, which he calls *Almost Type* 1. In the *Almost Type* 2, we would have Sisyphus pushing the stone up the hill, and reaching the top with great effort. Then, when Sisyphus has reached the top, instead of sitting back and taking a rest to enjoy the view, he sees that the top of the hill is also the beginning of another hill that had been hidden on the way up. He begins again to push the stone up the next hill, unaware that there could be yet a third hill awaiting him.

Monsignor Roberto is a good example of this; he no sooner finishes his visitation of the parish than he begins to prepare his homily for the next day. There is always the next job to be done and so he *almost* finishes for the day, only to discover something else to be done.

Conclusion

The combination of Process Script and driver behaviour helps give a more accurate picture of our behaviour on a day-to-day basis. It is worth spending time alone in order to allow ourselves to reflect deeply on our behaviour patterns. Self-reflection is a powerful door to self-understanding, and combined with gentle feedback from the people who know us best, this personal scrutiny will provide us with a more complete picture of our way of being in the world and of our personality type.

CHAPTER TWELVE

A Bird's Eye View

"The trick to forgetting the big picture is to look at everything close-up."
Chuck Palahniuk

Before we examine in the next Chapter how the various personality adaptations interact with each other, we take a moment in Chapter 12 to have an overview of the whole system of this personality typology (Kahler,

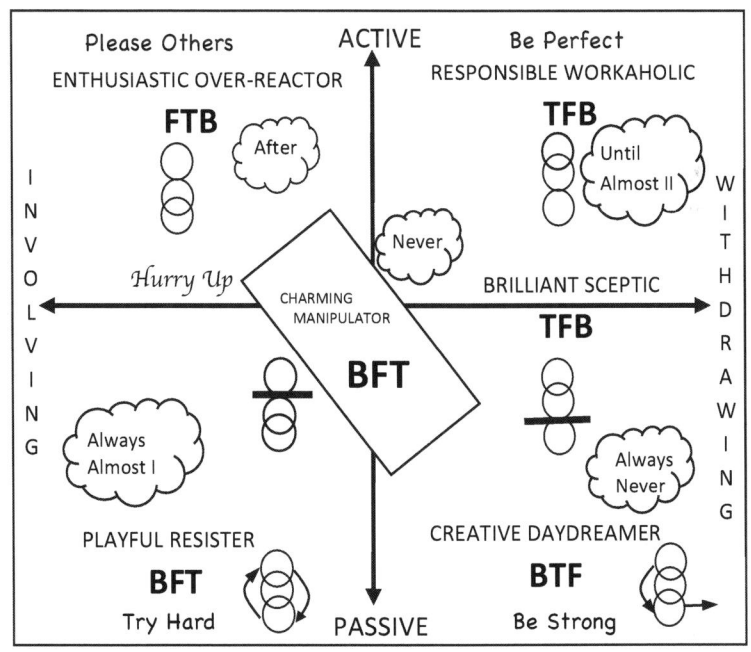

Fig. 12 A Bird's Eye View (Kahler, 1979; Joines & Stewart 2002)

1979; Joines & Stewart, 2002,205).

In Fig. 12 we have all the elements for each personality we have discussed in the previous chapters, and now we can view them as an interrelated system that has its own logic. For instance, you will notice that all the personality adaptations are situated in relation to the *x* and *y-axes*. We will begin by examining this type of positioning of the adaptations.

The Axes

The *y-axis* moves from the active to the passive way of reacting to our environment. In the active section, we have the Responsible Workaholic and the Enthusiastic Over-Reactor. We would expect, therefore, that both these personalities be more inclined to take the initiative or be more pro-active in relation to the challenges of life. They are the *doers* as opposed to the Creative Daydreamer and the Playful resister at the other end of the *y-axis* who are more inclined to follow than to lead.

The Brilliant Sceptic and the Charming Manipulator are at the mid-point. This indicates for the Brilliant Sceptic a certain tendency to cast a critical eye on people and events instead of entering fully into active engagement. At times, Brilliant Sceptics can sit on the fence and pontificate somewhat on the situations and people they are judging without taking any action. The Charming Manipulator likewise moves from a more active position to a more passive one, depending on his or her ability to manipulate the situation.

Then on the *x-axis*, we have the continuum from a withdrawing reaction to people right over to an involving approach.

The Brilliant Sceptic, the Responsible Workaholic and the Creative Daydreamer are more inclined to favour activity rather than relationships. So, they are more private, more introverted if you like, content to be alone for considerable amounts of time, and do things on their own. They withdraw from engaging with others.

The Charming Manipulator, the Enthusiastic Over-Reactor, and the Playful Resister, on the other hand, are situated towards the involvement end of the *x*-axis. While the Enthusiastic Over-Reactor is often energetically engaged in interpersonal interaction, the Playful Resister likes to be with people, but often he or she will hover on the outskirts of the crowd, happy to let the Enthusiastic Over-Reactor play the major part (Joines & Stewart, 2002). The Charming Manipulator moves from active involvement to a certain withdrawal. When things are going well for the Charming Manipulator, she or he is fine, but when things fall apart and Charming Manipulators are not getting what they want, then they retreat and move towards the withdrawal side of the *x*-axis.

The behaviours of each of the personality types span the continuum of active and passive behaviours and the corresponding levels of involvement and withdrawal. The challenge facing each of the personality adaptations is to move towards the opposite tendency in order to achieve greater balance. So, the Creative Daydreamers and Playful Resisters need to move towards the active quadrants, while the Responsible Workaholics and the Brilliant Sceptics need to become more relaxed and dwell a while in the passive areas. Likewise, with the Responsible Workaholics, the Sceptics and Creative Daydreamers, they need to become more sociable, while the Enthusiastic

A Bird's Eye View

Over-Reactors and Playful Resisters need to spend some time alone to allow them to reflect more on their behaviour.

Personality Adaptation	Description of the Behaviours
Creative Daydreamer	They withdraw into their own world, and wait there until invited to come out.
Brilliant Sceptic	They are suspiciously distrustful of people and events, and look for the problems before they can trust in the solution.
The Charming Manipulator	They are always plotting and planning in order to get what they want by hook or by crook.
The Responsible Workaholic	They will keep working to achieve the perfect outcome, and often find their value in what they achieve.
The Enthusiastic Over-Reactor	They are reactive emotionally, and will frequently act out without really thinking of the real consequences of their actions.
The Playful Resister	They resist any person whom they think is trying to control them, and may sometimes sabotage a project which they have undertaken.
Table 3. The Behaviour Doors of the Personality Adaptations	

Seeing how behaviours of each personality adaptation differ from each other, we can respond to these behaviours in appropriate ways. Failure to appreciate the differences can mistakenly lead us to treat people in ways that will not lead to effective communication, and may stereotype the various personality adaptations in a way that is not helpful. By way of summary, we outline these significant behavioural differences in Table 3 above.

Personality Adaptation	Description of the Feelings
The Creative Daydreamer	I manage my scare at being too much for my parents by hiding my feelings, and soothing myself through fantasy and creativity. I show I am strong.
The Brilliant Sceptic	I often appear to feel righteous and clever while often secretly feeling anxious that things won't work out. Basically, I don't trust people to do the job properly and so I'll do it myself.
The Charming Manipulator	I hide my feelings of abandonment by abandoning the person first so as to hide my pain and loneliness.
The Responsible Workaholic	I frequently hide my feelings of anxiety and sadness with a certain angry rigidity or over-control of any emotion.
The Enthusiastic Over-Reactor	I can display either anger to hide my sadness, or sadness to hide my anger, or laughter to cover everything.
The Playful Resister	I hide my anger and vengeful feelings by becoming passive or by using alcohol or drugs or food to prevent me from feeling at all.

Table 4. The Feeling Doors of the Personality Adaptations

Then, if we take the feeling door, we can see that many of the personality adaptation reveals a 'substitute feeling' that often masks their real authentic feelings

A Bird's Eye View

(Table 4). Alternatively, they control their feelings with a *Be Strong* driver so that they do not feel. So, like the behaviours above, the feelings associated with each of the personality adaptations vary from one group to the next.

Recognising the position of the thinking door and acknowledging the manner of thinking for each adaptation

Personality Adaptation	Description of the Thinking
The Creative Daydreamer	They are continually reflecting and analysing their situation in a personal and private way.
The Brilliant Sceptic	They are highly alert and analytical, seeking to discover the flaws or problems in any situation.
The Charming Manipulator	They are continually thinking about future projects and how they can get people to give them what they want. They are masters at strategizing to achieve their aims
The Responsible Workaholic	They find it difficult to stop obsessing, and are continually thinking about what next they have to do.
The Enthusiastic Over-Reactor	They spend a lot of time thinking on the ways they were not recognised, or were hurt or ignored.
The Playful Resister	They find themselves often confused and unclear in their thinking. They struggle to express themselves in a way that others clearly understand.

Table 5. The Thinking Doors of the Personality Adaptations

will give a clue as to the best way to engage with the personality adaptation in question (Table 5 above).

Needless to say, when the thinking door is the trapdoor, the only effective strategy is to avoid basing our interventions on a purely rational basis, and focus on either behaviours or feelings.

The Place of Time

This Chapter explains the way the various personality adaptations live out their Script in time. There are just a few clarifications that can be helpful in understanding the processes of some of the adaptation.

I refer to the Almost I and Almost II Process Scripts that are involved in the Playful Resister and the Responsible Workaholic respectively. Whereas the *Almost I* Script in the Playful Resister leads to a marred or imperfect outcome, the *Almost I* Script in the Responsible Workaholic only refers to the fact that the person with the Responsible Workaholic adaptation completes their task perfectly, and then realizes that they are only *almost* finished. They do not have the *Almost I* of the Playful Resister where the outcome is imperfect. It is only *Almost I* to the extent that the Responsible Workaholic is not finished when one job is completed. They are driven to strive for further perfection. Hence they have the *Almost II* Script.

With regard to the *Never* Script of the Charming Manipulator and the Creative Daydreamer, there is a slight difference in the quality of the *Never* Script in these two adaptations. The Charming Manipulator thinks wrongly that they will never get what they want by asking directly for it. However, they often succeed in getting what they want by stealth or dishonesty. In other words, they actively pursue what they want even if it is by foul means.

The Creative Daydreamer, on the other hand, is more resigned to the fact that they may *never* obtain their desired goal, and so they withdraw to nurse their sense of loss. They are more in touch with their sadness than with their justified anger, while the Charming Manipulator is more in touch with their anger that often covers their sadness.

Finally, with regard to the *Always* Script connected to the Playful Resister and the Creative Daydreamer, it is probably accurate to say that both Scripts reveal a certain passivity and resignation that contribute to a lack of determination to change their situation.

Conclusion

The other elements in Fig. 12 on page 113 (the contaminations and exclusions) are adequately covered in the relevant sections of each of the personality adaptations, and therefore there is no need to deal with them here.

I hope that the above comments will contribute to a clearer understanding of each of the adaptations, and provide a firm basis for exploring how each of the personality adaptations relates with the others. We will deal with this aspect of personality adaptations in the following Chapter.

CHAPTER THIRTEEN

It Takes All Sorts

"Variety's the spice of life, that gives it all its flavour."
William Cowper

The fact that personality adaptations differ significantly one from the other raises the question as to how they relate with each other, and how they combine within the one person. When one adaptation has feelings as the open door, how do they connect with the one who has feelings as the trapdoor? It certainly takes all sorts to make liquorice as the advertisement goes for Bassets sweets!

In this Chapter, we will reflect on how the personality adaptations view each other and combine with each other. As stated already in Chapter 2, we all have at least one surviving adaptation and one performing adaptation. So, here we will take each of the Surviving Adaptations and link them with the various performing adaptations with whom they relate, or with whom they join in the creation of a person's overall personality (Joines, 1986:152-160; Joines & Stewart, 2002).

Creative Daydreamer and Playful Resister

Certainly, the Creative Daydreamer (surviving adaptation) finds it quite easy to relate to the Playful Resister (performing adaptation) because of the latter's laid-back and non-threatening attitude. The passivity of the Playful Resister does not pose a threat to the way that the Creative Daydreamer withdraws and reveals a certain level of dissociation. So, it is easy to imagine that these two personalities could comfortably get on with each other, sharing in a spirit of 'live and let live'.

Needless to say however, when the combination of the surviving and performing adaptations comes together in the one person, we find a personality that is much inclined to become a passive member of a group, failing to play their part in any cooperative activity. In addition, the combination can lead to a certain level of intransigence where stubborn resistance (the performing adaptation) is combined with active withdrawal (surviving adaptation), making it difficult at times to bring the person out of their rebellion. Furthermore, because of their passivity, it is often difficult to know what is going on behind their lack of engagement.

At the same time, this combination can also go to create a personality that is generally gentle, non-threatening and playful. They can become valuable members of a community or group because of their desire for peace and harmony. Because they are not a threatening presence, they can smooth over troubled waters and promote a spirit of reconciliation.

Creative Daydreamer and Enthusiastic Over-Reactor

Sometimes this contrast makes for strained relationships since the trapdoor of the Creative Daydreamer is their feelings, which they find difficult to express until they have thought things out. The Enthusiastic Over-Reactor (performing adaptation), on the other hand, is so expressive that the Creative Daydreamer can find them over-powering to the point of feeling engulfed by the strength of their emotional power.

As the diagram on page 113 shows, (Fig. 12) the Enthusiastic Over-Reactor and the Creative Daydreamer are at opposite poles of the Process Matrix, which, of course, can have a positive outcome when we think that opposites often attract. The fact that the Creative Daydreamer 'hides' their emotions can lead them to admire the spontaneity of the Enthusiastic Over-Reactor.

When both qualities are in the same person we have someone who is often the life and soul of the party, full of fun and games, and yet can afterwards withdraw and even become depressed after the highs of the party celebrations. It seems that they can enjoy themselves, and then feel that they have to pay for their moment of freedom. Many a comedian displays this combination of public exuberance and private depression.

Creative Daydreamer and Responsible Workaholic

The Creative Daydreamer may be daunted by the focus and energy of the Responsible Workaholic. When they see the amount of work that the Responsible Workaholic undertakes, the Creative Daydreamers find themselves lost in their apparent inability to take initiatives and work to specific goals. They often feel inferior to the Responsible Workaholic and can, at times, feel dismissed by the Responsible Workaholic's impatience with the Creative Daydreamer's lack of drive or energy. Since the Creative Daydreamer is more focused on *being* than on *doing,* this combination can make for difficult bedfellows. They are at opposite extremes of the active-passive continuum

When however the Creative Daydreamer and Responsible Workaholic come together in the one person, this combination of personality adaptations makes for people who are compassionate and thoughtful in their wish to help others. They are often hard-working, anxious to complete tasks, and willing to be alone as they strive to achieve tangible results. They can stay for days on end alone in their rooms writing papers, or planning programmes, unaffected by the fact that they have little human contact. Their creativity and depth of feelings combine to make for people who are committed to the wellbeing of humanity.

This combination goes to create a hard-working, gentle and compassionate person, ever willing to help others, and dedicated in achieving noble goals and fostering inspiring ideals.

Brilliant Sceptic and the Enthusiastic Over-Reactor

Often the Brilliant Sceptic will find it rather difficult to interact with the Enthusiastic Over-Reactor because he or she will judge the emotional reactions of the Enthusiastic Over-Reactor to be disproportionate and lacking any real substance. Frequently, Brilliant Sceptics become impatient with what they consider to be emotional blackmail by the Enthusiastic Over-Reactor's games to gain attention. The rational approach of the Brilliant Sceptic will further escalate the reactions of the Enthusiastic Over-Reactor who will view the rational approach as unsympathetic, harsh and judgemental. Consequently, both parties can arrive at a difficult impasse where both feel resentful about the behaviour of the other.

Were both adaptations to be within the same person, we could have an explosive reaction with the brilliance of

Don't Talk to the Wall!

the Sceptic reacting over emotionally to situations that the Brilliant Sceptic considers inadequate or inappropriate. The razor sharp mind combined with a high emotional charge could be devastating for anyone within reach! On the other hand, were the two adaptations to work together in areas of injustice, the passion of the Over-Reactor together with the eloquence of the Sceptic could be a force to reckon with, and a real power for social change.

Brilliant Sceptic and Responsible Workaholic

These two adaptations form a real partnership and together they achieve amazing feats! They both have a strong thinking dimension, and consequently this twosome would be unbeatable when confronting a task that requires intellectual sophistication. However, on an *emotional* level they could create an intensity that could sabotage or block them. This partnership could create paralysis by analysis. Being so intelligent, they can see every angle of a problem and then find themselves stuck in managing their compulsion to get it perfectly right. The anger of the Responsible Workaholic, and the anxiety of the Brilliant Sceptic can so overwhelm them that they arrive at situations where they reach an impasse. Furthermore, because of their paranoia that leads them to believe that people are out to trick or cheat them, and their obsessive attention to every detail in a project or problem, they become stuck instead of advancing their plans.

The combination of the surviving Brilliant Sceptic and the performing Responsible Workaholic in the one person paints the picture of the responsible, hard-working and

It Takes All Sorts

efficient manager who is able to hold many portfolios with ease and effectiveness. You certainly can fully depend on them to carry out whatever task they undertake. The main difficulty of these combined adaptations is that their emotional development can easily be arrested by over-dedication to work, achievement and the drive for perfection. They need to develop an emotional life that balances their focus on doing and achieving. Without this, they will end up achieving a lot, but missing out on life.

Brilliant Sceptic and Playful Resister

Frequently these two adaptations find it difficult to get on with each other. The Brilliant Sceptic looks on the Playful Resister as a nuisance, someone who will never fully cooperate with them, or who will thwart their plans and projects through annoying passivity. The clarity of the Brilliant Sceptic finds the confusion of the Playful Resister's thinking processes frustrating. It seems that no matter how clearly the Brilliant Sceptic explains what needs to be done, the Playful Resister will fail to grasp what is meant. Moreover, no matter what opinion the Brilliant Sceptic has, it seems that the Playful Resister will have the opposite viewpoint.

The Playful Resisters, from their perspective, find the Brilliant Sceptic over-controlling, critical and frightening in their demand for accountability. They will avoid engaging with the Brilliant Sceptic, and as a performing adaptation, they will seek to 'do their own thing' despite the critical eye of this intolerant surviving adaptation.

The combination of the Brilliant Sceptic and the Playful Resister within the one person results in someone who seeks to get their own way come hell or high water.

They insist on their point of view even when it becomes obvious that they are wrong! Even though the Brilliant Sceptics' open door is thinking, their thinking can be limited by the levels of anxiety that underpin it. Then, when challenged, the Brilliant Sceptic can switch to the Playful Resister's process where the thinking is the trapdoor. Here the thinking becomes confused, contradictory and rather chaotic. Therefore, while the thinking process begins with clarity, it ends up in a mess of woolly thinking. This combination makes for a person who becomes difficult to work with since they continually seek to resist any form of real cooperation. It is often their way or the highway, and they will use the brilliance of their surviving adaptation and the resistance of their performing adaptation to oppose those who don't agree with them.

Charming Manipulator and Enthusiastic Over-Reactor

You see on the Process Matrix (Fig.12 on page 113) that the Charming Manipulator straddles the space of the Enthusiastic Over-Reactor (performing adaptation) and the Creative Daydreamer (surviving adaptation). When the Charming Manipulator is getting what they want, and are finding that people are willing to cooperate with their scheming, the Charming Manipulator is upbeat and enthusiastic. They are positive, energetic and productive. The charm and the enthusiasm of this surviving adaptation can be attractive and many a leader has these qualities that succeed in attracting people to follow them.

When the Charming Manipulator does not find people cooperative and open to their plans, the surviving adaptation can switch into the over-reaction of the performing adaptation, and can become vindictive, petty and argumentative. In this state the Charming Manipulator can act out in ways that are hurtful and bordering on the criminal. They become nasty and dangerous.

Often, the Charming Manipulator is attracted to the Enthusiastic Over-reactor because they find that they can easily manipulate them. Realising that Enthusiastic Over-Reactors need to please others, the Charming Manipulator turns on the charm to create a situation where Enthusiastic Over-Reactors feel that they are special in the eyes of this surviving adaptation. Since the Charming Manipulator likes the energy of the Enthusiastic Over-Reactor, this coupling of adaptations can work in a sort of manipulative way.

Charming Manipulator and Responsible Workaholic

These two adaptations are polar opposites. Whereas the Responsible Workaholic is dependable, upright and honest, the Charming Manipulator is inclined to be unreliable, somewhat devious and not always truthful. The philosophy of the Responsible Workaholic can be summarised in the phrase: 'They're my principles and I'm sticking by them!' The Charming Manipulator is more inclined to say: 'Them's (sic) my principles, and if you don't like them, I'll change them!' Hence, there is often suspicion and tension between these two adaptations, with the Responsible Workaholic reluctant to trust the Charming Manipulator, and feeling that they are being tricked all along the way. The Charming Manipulators, on the other hand, find the Responsible Workaholics rather rigid, too serious, and unwilling to take a chance.

When these two adaptations combine to form the one personality, we have a strange mixture. In many ways, it is unlikely that they could cohabit in the one person since they are polar opposites. These two adaptations have little in common, and even though they have the same target door of feelings, the quality of feelings differs considerably.

The anxiety of the Responsible Workaholic contrasts markedly with the sadness and rage of the Charming Manipulator. Their thinking open doors are different, the one clear and focussed, the other clouded and overly complicated.

Charming Manipulator and Playful Resister

The charm and the playfulness of these adaptations combine to create a certain fellowship between these two approaches to life. The dance between them involves the Charming Manipulator seeking to get what they want from someone who resists any form of control. The skill of the Charming Manipulator is such that they often manage to trick the Playful Resisters into allowing them to do what they want to do. Often Playful Resisters feel a certain resentment towards the Charming Manipulator, believing that Charming Manipulators always manage to get what they want, while the Playful Resisters find themselves stuck in the same situation, and often feel that they cannot change their circumstances.

When both adaptations combine in the one person we have a rather lethal concoction where the Charming Manipulator will resist any form of control and will use all their playful skills to get what they desire. Their charm and playfulness come together in the service of their scheming. Both adaptations have thinking as their trapdoor, and consequently, they will suppress their rational side in order to get what they want even when it become clear that this action is not wise. They undervalue rationality in favour of desire. When they want something, they don't bother about having to justify their actions, but simply take what they want irrespective of any moral issue.

Conclusion

In painting the characteristics of the surviving and performing adaptations, I may have given, at times, a rather negative portrait of some or all of the personalities. It is important to remember, however, that we all have each of the personality types within us. We all can be daydreamers, sceptics, manipulators, workaholics, over-reactors and resisters to a greater or lesser extent. Likewise, we can be creative, brilliant, charming, responsible, enthusiastic and playful. We are indeed a funny mixture of all of them! However, we normally favour one of the surviving adaptations and one or two of the performing adaptations.

It is also important to understand that we may have these personality types to a greater or lesser degree. Not all Playful Resisters are equally difficult to get to cooperate. Not all Brilliant Sceptics are totally paranoid. It depends on circumstance how much we invest in each of the types, and no two people are the same. We are all unique.

The fact that we are different one from the other implies that we communicate differently and we respond to others' communication in ways particular to our personality type or adaptation. In the next Chapter we see how channels of communication work with the various types, and how we can best connect with each of the personality types by using different channels of communication.

CHAPTER FOURTEEN

Channels Of Communication

*"You can change your world by changing your words...
Remember, death and life
are in the power of the tongue."*

Joel Osteen

How do we get on the wavelength of any of the personality types or adaptations? We all know that when we try to communicate with some people we find ourselves struggling to make contact, and often end up frustrated and mystified as to why we are not managing to communicate. Why should such a simple process of speaking and listening degenerate into an impasse of silence and deafness?

Taibi Kahler offers a useful model of communication that is intimately linked to the various personalities, and responsive to the particular needs of each person. (Kahler, 1979:4-10; 29). I will take the four of the channels that he links with the various personality types to explore how the use of these channels will assist in making our communication loud and clear.

The Directive Channel

It would appear that giving orders and issuing directives runs contrary to any real form of communication, and yet this approach seems to be effective particularly for the Creative Daydreamer and the Charming Manipulator when they are being passive.

By being directive with the Creative Daydreamer, we invite them to come out of their passivity and take action. Were we to wait until they volunteered to undertake a task, we would be waiting a long time. They are inclined simply to withdraw into themselves and engage in personal reflection. But such withdrawal often leads nowhere, and can be most frustrating when there are things to be done. Creative Daydreamers can have lovely thoughts and ideas but as someone said, 'Talk is cheap; it takes money to buy bread!' Unless words are followed by concrete action, little progress is made, and Creative Daydreamers remain in their ivory tower. When we are directive with Creative Daydreamers, we break through their passivity and invite them to action. The invitation is best made by issuing directives – literally telling them what to do. Unless they also have the performing adaptation of the Playful Resister, the Creative Daydreamer will respond well to our commands. If they do have a Playful Resister adaptation, we need to be wary of being so directive, and use other channels instead.

The Directive approach can also work initially with Charming Manipulators because it cuts through their scheming and plotting. By taking the direct approach, we give them a clear message about what we expect, and leave little leeway for wriggling out of a request. This directive approach needs, however, to be tempered with a warm and nurturing element, and this combination can break through the Charming Manipulator's resistances. Again, we stress that a directive approach will never work if the Charming Manipulator has a Playful Resister performing adaptation as well, since their main reaction to any control is to rebel against it.

The Requestive Channel

This approach works well for the Brilliant Sceptics and the Responsible Workaholics. Both of these personality types have thinking as their open door, and therefore, if you are clear as to what you want and why you want it, these two adaptations are likely to respond positively. Needless to say, we need to be precise as to exactly what we are requesting, and the rationale for the request. We cannot fudge the issue or present some half-baked ideas. But if we have things thought out clearly, the Responsible Workaholic will act responsibly, and be willing to shoulder another task despite a busy schedule. The Brilliant Sceptics, for their part, will trust that the person making the request does so for the benefit of a greater good, and therefore they will be willing to cooperate. Consequently, when we ask, 'Will you do this, please?' having explained the need you have, the likelihood is that the Brilliant Sceptics and the Responsible Workaholics will respond with a 'Yes'.

The Nurturative Channel

This approach touches into the emotional needs of the person being addressed, and makes contact at a feeling level. For the Enthusiastic Over-Reactor this is the ideal channel through we make contact as it responds to the needs this personality has for positive strokes. By nurturing Enthusiastic Over-Reactors we provide them with the love and acceptance that they continually seek, and that they respond to with warm appreciation. In fact, unless we are prepared to communicate through this channel, we may find ourselves up against a brick wall and a rather volatile one at that – if walls can be volatile! However, once we open this channel of communication with Enthusiastic Over-Reactors, we then can begin to deal with whatever matter is under discussion. You could say that this approach provides the key into the hearts of the Enthusiastic Over-Reactors, and fosters a spirit of companionship and mutual appreciation.

As mentioned above, the nurturative approach also works well with Charming Manipulators, and combined with the directive approach, it offers them a supportive and warm connection. Whereas the directive channel can be perceived as controlling and dominant, the ingredient of the nurturing softens this channel and responds to the Charming Manipulator's need to connect with their feelings.

The Emotive Channel

This is the channel that involves the sharing of feelings on the part of the listener and the speaker. By sharing feelings, both parties approach a level of intimacy that transforms the relationship. It is particularly with the Enthusiastic Over-Reactors that this channel works best. Their open door is through

Channels of Communication

their feelings, and as feelings are shared, the person is welcomed and accepted. By sharing feelings, both parties form a bond of friendship that transforms their *Please Other* driver into a reciprocity that gives life to both sides. Teasing and joking can also form part of the emotive channel and such behaviour can be equally effective in working with Enthusiastic Over-Reactors and Playful Resisters.

Both the nurturative and the emotive channels are indeed the channels that respond best to the needs of the Playful Resister. As they experience the warmth and acceptance of the other person, and the playful nature of the interaction, while feeling no pressure to perform in a particular way, they begin to react positively to this sense of unconditional positive regard.

Channels of Communication

Directive Channel	Creative Daydreamer
	Charming Manipulator
Requestive Channel	Responsible Workaholic
	Brilliant Sceptic
Nurturative Channel	Enthusiastic Over-Reactor
	Playful Resister
	Charming Manipulator
Emotive Channel	Enthusiastic Over-Reactor
	Playful Resister
	Charming Manipulator

Conclusion

The channels of communication respond suitably to the needs of the different personality adaptations or types. As we become familiar with each of the personalities, we can begin to test out Taibi Kahler's theory of the channels of communication. Ultimately, it is only as we practise using these channels that we will become proficient in shifting smoothly from one channel to the other according to the surviving or performing adaptations that we are addressing. At first, it may feel rather artificial using this approach. Some people argue that all we have to do is be ourselves as we communicate. However, such an approach fails to appreciate how different people are, and how varied people's needs are.

By using the channels of communication, we are recognizing the individuality of people, and beginning to adapt to their differences. It takes time and effort to develop this elegant approach to communication, but like any new task we have to learn, we move from conscious competence to unconscious competence (Burch, 1970). With practice we will find that our use of the channels becomes automatic as we come in contact with the various personality types. As we begin to experience the fruits of our efforts, we will grow in our ability to connect with all sorts of people in ways that lead to healthy and enriching relationships.

In the following Chapter, we examine the work of Bader and Pearson who offer an effective model of how best to be an 'Inquirer' as we seek to engage with a variety of personality adaptations. By using the various channels of communication and employing listening skills, we will facilitate the creation of healthy on-going interpersonal relationships that make for peaceful and fruitful dialogue.

CHAPTER FIFTEEN

Instead of Talking to the Wall

"We're all islands shouting lies to each other across seas of misunderstanding."
Rudyard Kipling

I hope that we have come to the point where we see that we have an alternative to talking to the wall! By understanding the characteristics of different personality types, and how they developed as a result of early family experiences, we can connect with people in the way that best suits them and honours their individuality. The channels of communication that I explained in Chapter 14, offer us various options that are appropriate to the different adaptations, and make for much easier interpersonal relationships.

However, communication is never that easy, and frequently we will come up against moments of conflict, moments of misunderstandings. Even when we approach someone through their open door, approach their target door, and use the best channel of communication, there is never any guarantee that things will automatically go that smoothly. In fact, the real challenge in communication is how we manage conflict and maintain our relationships. There will be times of disagreement in any human interaction, and we need, therefore, to acquire the skill of the '*Inquirer*' as outlined by the innovative work of Bader and Pearson, (http://www.couplesinstitute.com).

The Bader and Pearson Model

Dr Bader is a Transactional Analyst as well as someone who has specialised with her husband in the area of couple therapy. Doctors Ellyn Bader and Peter Pearson have proposed a method for conflict resolution, which I have adapted somewhat in the various workshops I run. What I intend to do in this Chapter is to take the approach they designed for conflict resolution, and apply it to the various personality types or adaptations. Although they have designed a process that involves the dual roles of the *Inquirer* and the *Initiator*, for the purpose of this book I will focus on the role of the *Inquirer*. I do this because I am convinced that if people learn to be true Inquirers, they will have overcome many of the difficulties involved in conflict management. People can study the role of the *Initiator* either by logging onto their website and purchasing some of their CDs or DVDs or reading *Are We Together?* (Gibson, 2014) where I deal with the role of the Initiator.

The Inquirer

In order to become an effective listener, Bader and Pearson emphasise the need for one of the parties to become what they term an '*Inquirer*'. Basically, the *Inquirer* is the one who is most open to listening intently to the other person. To listen well, the *Inquirer* has to accomplish four tasks, which I have slightly modified from the Bader and Pearson model by giving the process the title: 'The 2Cs and the 2Es", naming each task with easy-to-remember names. The 2Cs are: Be Calm and Be Curious. The 2Es are: Be Empathic and Be an Echo.

Be Calm

Imagine the challenge of managing the rage of an Enthusiastic Over-reactor who is liable even to physically attack you, or the rage of the Brilliant Sceptic who touches into your vulnerability with cold criticism. What about the frustration that mounts in you in the face of the passivity of the Playful Resister, or the lack of initiative of the Creative Daydreamer? As we interact with each of the personality types, our own adaptations will kick in, and often we can be angry, reactive and stressed as a result of our reaction to the other person's behaviour.

Anger and the stress often prevent the possibility of careful listening, and potentially make the situation of conflict worse. We build up our internal agitation and find that we have hit the wall, a wall we certainly cannot talk to.

The challenge therefore is to remain calm. This means that we need to seek first to understand the other person before even trying to respond with our own ideas (Covey, 1989). We need to avoid defending ourselves, arguing, or taking things personally. In a word, we need to STOP, be SILENT, SENSE what is happening inside us, and SEE the bigger picture, especially from the other's point of view. These 4Ss are helpful reminders that may keep us grounded when the storms are gathering!

For Enthusiastic Over-Reactors to remain calm when their feelings are hurt, or when they are undervalued or ignored is quite a challenge. It is only when they practise the 4Ss that they will manage to move towards their thinking door – to stop, be silent, sense what is going internally and see the bigger picture. Otherwise they will be inclined to react rather than respond from an Adult ego state.

The Brilliant Sceptics also face the challenge of maintaining their internal equilibrium when they see people behaving in ways they consider wrong, unjust or threatening. Instead of taking on the Critical Parent's voice, they need to soothe their inner critical voice, and pause before launching an unwarranted attack on an unsuspecting victim.

Remaining calm becomes essential for good interpersonal relationships, and it applies to each of the personality types. In a sense, each adaptation has its own particular challenge with regard to maintaining an inner emotional balance, and each person needs to recognize the various triggers that go to threaten his or her inner calm. In addition, as we interact with each of the personality adaptations, we need to be able to remain calm before the behaviour of the different personality types. Once we are calm, we can then become curious.

Be Curious

Curiosity can come either from the Free Child or the integrated Adult (see Chapter 3). When we are curious, we are focused on the world beyond us. We move from my world to your world, from my point of view to your viewpoint. Being curious involves asking questions that show we are keen to understand the other's experience. It is important not to assume that we immediately understand what the other person is saying, but seek clarification all along the way (Erskine, 1996:316ff).

From our understanding of the differences in each of the personality adaptations, we now realize that the various personality types view the world from individual perspectives. The Creative Daydreamers contemplate their reality from a place deep inside their being. This is different for the Charming Manipulators who meet reality head on, and seek to get what they want by whatever means they can devise. The same is true of all the personality types; they each have a frame of reference that is unique to their type (Schiff, 1975:50). Hence, there is need for us to be curious about their viewpoint. We cannot take it for granted that they have the same perspective on life that we do. By being curious, we open ourselves to *their* world and offer them the opportunity to express their hopes and desires that are peculiar to them. Curiosity involves asking open-ended questions that allow for the other person to explain their standpoint without us having our own views interrupting them.

The asking of questions is a real art, and requires considerable practice. Often, for instance, the 'Why?' question needs to be considered carefully as it can give the impression of an aggressive confrontation (Strachan, 2007: 24). The 'Why?' question is especially dangerous when feelings are running high, as it appears that people are being accused or blamed. So, instead of asking, 'Why did you do that?' and alternative could be, "What was your thinking when you decided to take that plan of action?' Somehow, this alternative question does not have the same edge as the 'Why?'

When we are curious, we invite the person to be open and without defences, and in touch with their real needs. The person then begins to grow in self-esteem, and increases their ability to relate on an Adult-Adult basis (Erskine, 1996:320).

Be Empathic

The first E of this Inquirer process is: Be Empathic. Empathic transactions involve the sending of an emphatic message to another person, with the other experiencing the message as empathic (Clark, 1991:312ff). The message is empathic when the other person experiences being understood and accepted.

The process has two parts wherein we express understanding of the other person's viewpoint, while, at the same time, the other person feels that he or she has been understood. Our capacity to mentalise involves the ability to perceive and respond to the people's emotional state, mirroring them, while becoming aware of our own emotional states, which may be different from the other person's (Allen & Fonagy, 2006:12). The phrase 'stand in the shoes of your brother or sister for a mile' is a challenging reminder of the need to see things from the other's point of view. When people feel that they have been heard, some of their defences drop, and they become more open to be self-reflective instead of being oppositional or reactive.

This level of attunement moves beyond empathy where the person enters into a process of communion and unity with the other person (Erskine, 1996: 316ff). It involves being aware both of the boundary between the other person and the self, and of the affect that one person has on the other person. This attunement is both affective and cognitive, involving feelings and thinking, as we recognise the relational needs of the other person (Ibid: 320). Such attunement validates the other person's thinking, feelings and behaviours in a way that the person recognises a presence that is supportive of their current state of mind. It is as if the person feels totally understood and accepted for *who* they are, and *how* they are in the moment. The result of such attunement is that the person feels free to reveal even more of their reality, which up to then they may have been defending against.

And in this intersubjective moment, we experience empathy, sympathy and identification with the other person. Such empathic moments are moments of real meeting (*Ibid*: 151).

Each of the personality adaptations responds well to such an empathic approach. Often it is by showing empathy that the other person is facilitated to move from their open door to the target door, until finally they uncover the riches of their trapdoor.

Be an Echo

The second E of the Inquirer process is: Be an Echo. This technique requires the listener simply to 'play back' what they have heard from the other person. In a way, what we feedback is a replay of what the person said, which lets the other person know that they have been heard accurately, both at a social level and especially at a psychological level (Berne, 1966, 227).

The main challenge at this stage is to be attuned to the person, and to enter into the world of the other person without our own agenda running. This is an Adult ego state position, where we concentrate on the

Instead of Talking to the Wall

here-and-now as we listen to what is being communicated (Erskine, 1996: 321). Often the person may present their experiences in some coded form, and the challenge often is to decode what is being said and get to the heart of what lies behind the social message (Berne, 1966:243).

We see in Fig. 13 that the process of conflict resolution invites us to move from being calm to being curious, and then to move to the empathic and echo stages. We call this process the 'Cycle of Inquiry'. This is not a linear process but rather something that is an iterative, cyclical dynamic that responds to the interpersonal interaction between differing personality types. Depending on the circumstances, we may move from one skill to the other in no particular order. And indeed, there may be times when we focus more on one or other of the Cycle of Inquiry. What is important to keep in mind is that each of the elements of the Cycle of Inquiry offers us a valuable technique in keeping the channels of communication open.

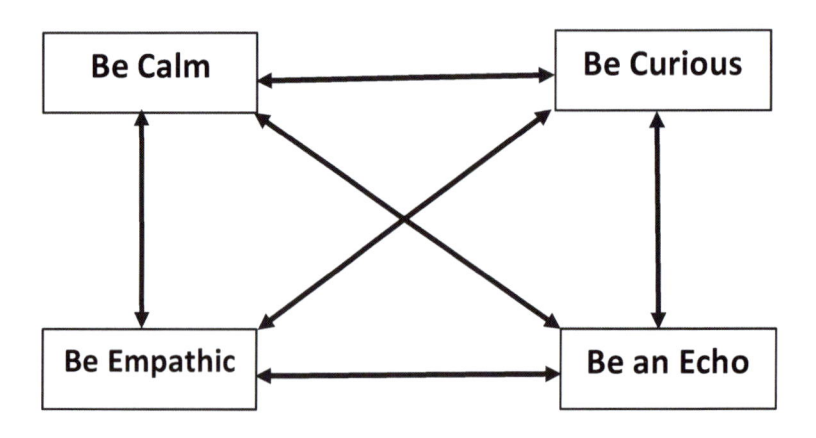

```
┌─────────────┐         ┌─────────────┐
│  Be Calm    │ ←─────→ │ Be Curious  │
└─────────────┘    ╳    └─────────────┘
┌─────────────┐         ┌─────────────┐
│ Be Empathic │ ←─────→ │  Be an Echo │
└─────────────┘         └─────────────┘
```

Fig. 13 The Cycle of Inquiry

However, it should be stressed again that the most important element in the role of the Inquirer is the Be Calm, for without achieving calm, our access to the other three elements is majorly compromised. Once we can stay calm and remain in Adult, we have the option to move to each of the other elements of the Cycle of Inquiry and be curious, empathic and an echo in the face of conflict or misunderstandings.

The challenge is to come to know the various personality adaptations or types so well that we automatically respond to each person in the manner that best mirrors their approach to life.

In any moment of conflict, we need to practise moving through each of the four elements of the Inquiry Cycle so that our responses become elegant interactions that show empathy and respect for the other person.

Conclusion

The challenge facing each of us in life is to connect with people, and to form circles of compassion where we view others with kindness and understanding. In a world often torn with strife, it becomes even more urgent to learn how to relate in a peaceful and non-violent way.

As we come to appreciate how different people are in their outlook, and how they uniquely express themselves, we are able to communicate openly and honestly in ways that respect individual differences.

CHAPTER SIXTEEN

Permissions

"Dream and give yourself permission
to envision a *you* that you choose to be."
Joy Page

Even though the personality types are not pathological as personality disorders are, they are still reactions to the conscious and unconscious messages that people received from their parents. In Chapter 4 we discussed the *drivers,* which we understood as messages that children picked up from their parents. These messages indicated that there were certain conditions to be fulfilled before children were considered OK. The five drivers of Kahler: *Be Perfect, Be Strong, Try Hard, Please Others* and *Hurry Up* set down the rules for children and laid the foundation for the creation of the personality types (Kahler, 1978:243). In Fig.12 (page 113) we can see where the *drivers* are connected to the various personality adaptations.

Allowers

As people begin to move towards the formation of an integrating Adult, they need to replace the *driver* behaviour with what Kahler calls '*allowers*' (Kahler, 1978:236). Kahler defined *allowers* in terms of permissions to disobey the *drivers,* where the person begins to feel OK without having to employ the *drivers.*

Allowers come from an unconditional OK life

position, whereas we saw that the drivers were messages from the parent to the child that the child was conditionally OK as long as they were perfect, strong, trying hard, pleasing others or hurrying up (Chapter 4).

The *allowers* send different messages to a person, and they may be sent by friends, colleagues, and relations as well as from the parents themselves. As opposed to the *driver* messages, the *allower* messages sound like: *It's Good Enough; Share your feelings; Just do It! Please yourself! Take your Time!* Each of the *allowers* facilitates the person to lessen the driven quality of their personality adaptations, and integrate the positive qualities contained in each personality type.

> ### *Allowers*
> 1. **It's good enough**
> 2. **Share your feelings!**
> 3. **Just do it!**
> 4. **Please yourself!**
> 5. **Take your time!**

As each of the *allowers* is presented, I think it important to state that these messages may have been sent by parents who displayed unconditional love for their children. Children who come from such families will obviously have more of the positive aspects of the personality adaptations and less of the negative qualities. Alternatively, these messages may also be sent by friends, relations or colleagues to adults who then grow and develop as a result of receiving these

Permissions

permissions or *allowers*. Hence, the reparative process of overcoming negative messages from our parents ensures that our personalities can grow and develop despite early negative experiences in our families.

A brief explanation of each of the *allowers* will show the positive impact of these permissions have on the development of the person.

It's Good Enough

This message of *It's Good Enough* allows children to make mistakes and learn from them. The parents of these children are not obsessed with detail, nor are they over demanding that their children be perfect. They guide their children calmly and in a relaxed manner, recognising that their children can do a good enough job. And they do not withdraw affection when their children fail; instead, they encourage them to get up and try again. Children's experience of parents who accept them unconditionally lays the foundations for a healthy level of self-esteem.

Adults who experienced this message in their childhood have a rather relaxed approach to life, and are aware that they will not get things perfect all of the time, and are willing to live with situations that may be less than ideal. They are not defensive when they make mistakes, and are tolerant of others who fail similarly.

The result of such a positive message in the *allower* means that the internal Critical Parent voice is replaced by a Nurturing Parent voice that gives permission for the person to exercise their Free Child (see Chapter 3).

Share your Feelings!

When parents substitute the *allower, Share your Feelings,* instead of the *driver* message of *Be Strong*, they are willing to accept their children when they are sad, angry or afraid, and are prepared to listen to their children without unnecessarily reassuring them. These parents allow their children express their feelings in a free and easy manner. The parents recognise that the child's feelings are unique to that child, and in accepting the children's feelings, the parents are communicating to their children that they are OK especially when they express difficult or uncomfortable feelings. In other words, instead of the message 'Be Strong!', they encourage their children to acknowledge that their feelings are their friends.

Children who grow up knowing that they can freely express their feelings are more likely to engage with people instead of withdrawing into their shells. They seem as adults to have an innate ability to experience a wide repertoire of emotions in the space of a day. They allow themselves naturally to move from one feeling to the next depending on the situation, and no emotion is out of bounds. They can be spontaneous in response to the differing situations in which they find themselves. As a result, people come to know them as they are, and can therefore feel confident that they get what they see in the other person. There is no attempt on the part of the adult to hold back their feelings or to modulate them out of fear of what others will think when they express exactly what they feel. As a result, these people come across as well balanced, integrated and mature.

Just Do It!

Since the Try Hard driver is the result of over-controlling parents, the parents who allow their child to complete tasks are those parents who avoid any sense of excessive control. They celebrate when their child accomplishes a task, and don't just accept the fact that the child tried but did not finish the job. So, the parent does not bribe the child to do the work, nor does the parent readily accept unfinished or sloppily completed duties. The child soon learns that actions speak louder than words, and that often words are excuses for actions that have not been completed. Parents call their children to be accountable for their responsibilities, but in a spirit of love and acceptance.

Adults who have experienced such parents are inclined to achieve much. It is not that they feel driven like the Responsible Workaholic, but they simply enjoy the 'buzz' or sense of achievement when they have completed a task. They come across as conscientious, well organised, careful and methodical. People rely on them to do a job properly, and invariably they find that this type of person will not let them down. People with the *allower, Just Do It!,* often display high energy and positivity in any task they approach. They enjoy the challenge of undertaking projects that will require concentration, care and commitment.

Please Yourself!

The parents, who demand that their children please them in order for the child to be accepted, are different from the parents who encourage their children to live their lives independently, and not simply to please them.

The child grows up, not constantly wondering if everything they do pleases or displeases their parents or other people. Instead, the child picks up the message that they need to do things not just to please others, but because they want to do them, and because in doing them, they can please themselves, and achieve what they want in life.

Adults who feel free to please themselves are liberated from the guilt of having always to please others. This does not mean that these people are selfish or unconcerned about others. Rather they are able to say 'no' when they want to say 'no'. Instead of having always to say 'yes' out of a compulsion to please others, these adults feel free to decide what they will do, and what they do not want to do.

This level of freedom means that these adults feel in control of their lives in a mature and healthy way. They appear grounded in the manner by which they interact with others, and show a level of common sense that is not dependent on how they think others might judge or criticize them.

Take your Time!

Relaxed parents make for relaxed children. Relaxed children are not synonymous with lazy children, or procrastinators. The message 'take your time' offers children the space to go at their own pace, and to complete a job properly without the pressure to 'hurry up'. Unlike the 'hurry up' person, the actual doing of the job for the relaxed person is more significant than the end point. In a sense, the journey becomes more important than the destination.

Permissions

Often Charming Manipulators have an element of the *Hurry Up driver, which* lands them into trouble when they do not think out carefully the various schemes that they plot. Adults, on the other hand, with the *allower* that encourages them to focus on the task, find that they live in the present moment as they work on a project, and are willing to be engrossed in the doing of the work as they are in completing it. The permission to take the necessary time for whatever they have in hand leaves these adults calm, focused and methodical.

Conclusion

We all have our personality adaptations with their concomitant *drivers.* Few people have grown up in families where parents did not impose certain conditions of behaviour on their children in order for the children to gain acceptance and love.

However, the journey to a more wholesome way of living is to lessen the power of the personality adaptations and to develop the positive side of each of them. Hence, the work of each person is to develop their creativity, their thinking, their sense of responsibility as well as their enthusiasm, their ability to be charming and their freedom to play! By practising the behaviours associated with the *allowers*, adults become the sort of integrated person that is self-aware, spontaneous and capable of being intimate (Berne, 1964:158).

CHAPTER SEVENTEEN

Transformation

"Personal transformation can and does have global effects. As we go, so goes the world, for the world is us. The revolution that will save the world is ultimately a personal one."
Marianne Williamson

So far I have explained how personality adaptations were formed through the experience of children feeling that they could only be acceptable if they adapted to the wishes of their parents, significant others and the surrounding culture. With the formation of personality adaptations, children carry this mechanism into adulthood where they continue to behave in adapted ways in order to feel OK with themselves and others.

But the challenge facing each of us is to become free and vibrant people, unlimited in our capacity to love and be loved, to express ourselves in the moment without any fear of what others might think, and to respond to life with spontaneity and self-awareness. In fact, Eric Berne defined autonomy as our capacity to be self-aware, spontaneous and intimate, qualities that do not require us to adapt in ways that limit our freedom (*Ibid.* 158). When we are autonomous, we are free of any psychological adaptations. Or rather, as Joines

Transformation

commented in a private communication, we do not aim simply to rid ourselves of the adaptations, but instead we focus on developing the positive side of the adaptation while allowing the negative side to diminish (Joines, 2014: personal communication).

The Reason for the Adaptations

The personality types that we have learnt to assume are restrictive ways of behaving for the sake of managing our early life experiences. They were the best solutions to rather difficult circumstances, and they certainly worked at the time of their formation in childhood. By becoming a Playful Resister we managed the situation where our parents were over-controlling, dominant and/or engulfing. The same was true of the Creative Daydreamers who found that by taking care of themselves, and not stressing out their parents by asking for what they needed, they were able to remain somewhat tranquil and not burdensome. The same can be said for each of the personality adaptations; each one created a method of managing their early childhood experiences, and by so doing formed a way of negotiating their journey through life. Their surviving adaptation got them over the moments of real stress, and the performing adaptations ensured that their parents affirmed them.

Adaptations – Our Response to Parents

Another way of expressing it is to say that each of the personality adaptations was our best effort at developing into the person we were required by our parents to be. Yet because they were adaptations that we made in response to our parental influences, they do not adequately represent the potential that is within each of us to be fully human and fully alive.

We have also said that we have all of the personality types within us, even if we give major emphasis on one of the surviving adaptations and one of the performing adaptations. By this I mean that there is a level of creativity, of charm and of brilliance in each of us. Likewise, there is also an element of daydreaming, scepticism and manipulation as part of our behaviour. When we are seeking approval, we want people to see us as responsible, enthusiastic and playful, even if we have to over-work, over-react and over-resist in order to achieve these qualities!

The question, therefore, remains: how do we live our lives without the need to adapt to the views, opinions and dictates of others? How can we be authentic without the need to be stuck in a particular personality type?

Personality Typologies

When we think of the Myers-Briggs personality test, the challenge facing each person is how to balance the dualities of extroversion-introversion, intuitive-sensing, thinking-feeling and perception-judgement (Myers, 1980:2959). As people develop their type fully, they come face to face with the obvious deficits of that particular type. The work they need to undertake, therefore, consists in addressing the lacunae in their personal make-up so that they can have a greater balance in the Jungian dualities.

The Enneagram personality typology offers another

Transformation

very valuable way to classify the way people interact with the world and with each other. It identifies nine personality types, giving each personality a number from one to nine. Each number is characterized by particular ways of thinking, feeling and behaviour. For instance, the one is the perfectionist, while the two is the helper. The three is the person who seeks success at all costs, while the number fours see themselves as special or unique. Each number focuses on the specific compulsion that characterizes the person. So, in a sense, the Enneagram identifies the basic flaw in a person's character. With the Enneagram, the invitation to each person with a specific number is to move to a complementary number that will ensure the redemption of their compulsive number (Fig. 14). So, for instance, the number one perfectionist is invited to move to the good qualities of the number seven who is more playful and spontaneous, and less emotionally bound to the tyranny of perfection (Riso & Hudson, 1999:121).

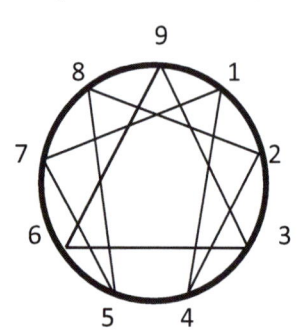

Fig. 14 The Enneagram

How to move towards Autonomy

This movement from our present limited psychological freedom to a place of greater autonomy is by no means an easy problem to solve. How does the introvert become more extrovert? How does the passive number nine in the Enneagram move towards the achieving and successful number three? And how do Charming Manipulators learn to ask directly for what they want without engaging in all sorts of scheming?

Progressive Mental Alignment

Jacob Korthuis, a Dutch health and medical practitioner has devised a fascinating method of confronting our various traumas that caused us to develop our personality types or adaptations (Korthuis, 2006). He calls this method Progressive Mental Alignment (PMA).

Korthuis stresses the intimate connection between our brains and our bodies, demonstrating that any experience (he calls these 'clusters') triggers activity both in the brain and in the body. When a person has a negative experience, their brain manages the pain of the event by focusing on a small element of the experience, leaving all the other elements of the experience – sub clusters - and the emotions connected with these sub-clusters in their unconscious. Then, because the event is traumatic, they often suppress the memory of the event, and it goes into their subconscious and may not emerge for many years. However, even though they have assigned the main event to their subconscious, they are often controlled by the physiological impact of many of the other elements of the event that they did not focus on during the trauma. These are the 'bad' clusters, which are connected to the high stress levels of the original event. So, they may feel the effects of the event, but do not have a clear idea of what happened because

Transformation

of having suppressed it. As a result of having all these elements in their unconscious, they find that when one of these sub clusters repeats itself in their lives – it may be a smell, a sound, a colour etc. - they immediately feel all the strong feelings from the original trauma in a situation that has nothing to do with the current event. So, theoretically they could have a panic attack when they sit down on a green bench and wonder what caused this attack. What they do not realize is that they suffered a real trauma when they were three years old as they sat on a green bench!

Progressive Mental Alignment involves a technique whereby people can go back to the 'bad cluster' and get in contact with those elements that they had hidden in their unconscious. By so doing, the physiological impact of the event disappears.

It is beyond the scope of this book to describe in detail the work of Korthuis, but I find it fascinating that we could have the possibility of bringing to consciousness the effects of traumas that caused the formation of our personality adaptations or types.

The work of Korthuis could have a major impact on the transformation of personality adaptations, and could offer people a simple yet effective way to clear their baggage from the past. His claim is that PMA will release the full power of possibility we all have inside of us. Personally, I look forward to developing this aspect of my work in helping people let go of their personality adaptations in the service of freedom and authentic living.

Redecision Therapy

Bob and Mary Goulding, followers of Eric Berne and Fritz Perls, devised a process called 'Redecision Therapy' when they helped clients go back into their personal history and discover the decisions that they made in as a result of their negative experiences in the home (Goulding & Goulding, 1979). Having identified the event that caused clients to be stuck in their lives, by the use of two-chair-work and other techniques, the Gouldings invited the client to get in contact with the early life decision they made, and then to change that decision in order to liberate the person from the trauma of the past.

Our Script and Transactional Analysis

Eric Berne himself talked about how as children we wrote a Script that made sense to us when we were young (Berne, 1972). In the face of our childhood experiences, we made up a story or Script that helped us manage our lives. The problem with this Script is that, while it worked in the past, it no longer helps us live our lives freely and joyfully. Hence, Berne created Transactional Analysis to help people change their Script. He believed that through the analysis of our ego states, our transactions with other, the psychological games we play, and the Script we create, we could change our lives to become autonomous human beings (Berne, 1964).

The Changes We Make

As we look at each of the personality types, we can clearly identify what sort of behavioural changes

Transformation

indicate that transformation is taking place. Needless to say, making these changes requires determination and perseverance. However, once a person understands the value of focusing on the positive aspects of the personality types, he or she can begin to make conscious choices to live life differently.

Creative Daydreamers

Creative Daydreamers will take a more active part in life, emerging out of their cocoon of comfort or fear to engage actively in interpersonal relationships. They will express their feelings more readily and risk relying on others instead of continuing to act independently. They will allow their Child ego state to emerge instead of hiding behind their belief that they are too much for others to handle. Moreover, they will begin to volunteer to undertake tasks without people having to drag them into action.

Brilliant Sceptics

Brilliant Sceptics will be more trusting and less critical of others. They will get in touch with the Nurturing Parent that will soothe their anxiety, and give them a sense that things will work out as they hope they will. Instead of being critical of other's ideas, they will affirm what is good and possible in other's suggestions, and then add further ideas to improve them. Instead of seeing the obstacles in everything, they will be more trusting, and come to see the possibilities in the opportunities that come their way. In short, they will be more positive and trusting about life, and less guarded in their approach to people and situations.

Charming Manipulators

Charming Manipulators will ask for what they want directly, prepared to be disappointed at times when they do not get what they want, and live with the resulting disappointment. They will understand the difference between manipulation and strategizing, where the former is dishonest and the latter simply a valuable way to communicate their ideas. Honesty will replace their secretive way of acting. When, therefore, they do not get what they want, they will stay with their feelings of disappointment instead of reacting like a spoilt child.

Responsible Workaholics

Responsible Workaholics will be prepared to take it easy, and to silence their Critical or Controlling Parent when the Parent voice of blame begins to emerge. They will begin to be gentle on themselves, taking suitable breaks from their busy schedule, penciling in moments of relaxation in their diaries so as not to become overwhelmed with work. They will allow themselves to make mistakes and not beat themselves up when they mess up. They will also begin to forgive their parents for being so harsh on them when they were young. In addition, they will nurture their sense of humour and begin to enjoy life.

Enthusiastic Over-Reactors

Enthusiastic Over-Reactors will become more reflective when they begin to feel strongly when they feel they have been ignored or slighted. They will pause instead of immediately reacting to the times or situations when they feel hurt. They will become more compassionate and understanding of others who may have different ideas to them. They will begin to allow other people to take centre stage while they become content simply to stay more in the background.

Playful Resisters

Playful Resisters will pay more attention to the ideas of others, especially the ideas of those they feel are too strong or too controlling. They will focus on the ideas of these people instead of reacting to their sense that these people are too powerful and dominant. They will cooperate when people ask them directly to undertake a job, and will be more careful in carrying out their duties. They will begin to plan more diligently and take action instead of procrastinating. When they feel resentful, they will begin to share their resentments and hurts instead of acting them out, or harbouring them secretly.

These are just some of the observable changes that we can expect to see when people begin to loosen their hold on their personality adaptations.

Affirmations

Louise Hay's Book, *You Can Heal Your Life* (1984) stressed the value of repeating affirmations as a way of changing our way of thinking, feeling and behaving. She believed that affirmations could change our way of thinking which in turn would modify our behaviour and our feelings. For her, a thought was simply a thought and therefore could be transformed (Hay, 1984:xiii).

Moreover, she posited that our subconscious mind accepts whatever we choose to believe (*ibid.* 2).

While some question the power of affirmations, I think it could be of value to explore the sorts of affirmations that the various personality types could employ to loose the hold of the negative aspects of each type, and develop the more positive side of them. So, for example, what sort of affirmations could develop the responsible aspect of the Responsible Workaholic while avoid its compulsive nature. My belief is that if we focus on developing the more positive side of the personality type, the other more negative side will adjust accordingly.

As an experiment, I suggest the following affirmations for the various personality types and encourage you, the reader, to develop your own affirmations that may help your journey towards personal transformation.

Creative Daydreamer

- I value the connection I can have with people
- Sharing my feelings with others is a risk worth taking
- I have an important part to play in the drama of life
- My ideas are worth sharing with others
- My creativity brings colour to an otherwise drab world

Brilliant Sceptic

- I begin to see what is right with other people's ideas
- I trust

- I listen with openness to what people tell me
- I believe that things will work out for the best
- I am calm and relaxed

Charming Manipulator

- I ask for 100% of what I want 100% of the time
- I say 'yes' when I want to say 'yes'
- I say 'no' when I want to say 'no' (Joines, 2002)
- I express my needs directly with without fear
- I love the truth which will set me free

Responsible Workaholic

- I take time for myself instead of working non-stop
- I can do a good enough job
- My life is more important than my work
- I have a right to exist and to enjoy life
- I am good enough as I am

Enthusiastic Over-Reactor

- Whenever people criticise me, I don't take it personally
- I check out any fantasies or resentments I may have
- I pause and reflect when I have strong feelings
- Feelings and reality are not always in sync
- I avoid making assumptions

Playful Resister

- I see life is full of possibilities
- I work with ease and competence
- I do today what calls for immediate action
- When I feel I'm being controlled, I open my mind to others' ideas

- I consider all the options when considering a choice of action

Discovering our Script

For changes to take place in the various personality types, people will need to get in touch with the underlying Script that has led to the development of such behaviours. Behaviours are simply the symptoms of a deeper dynamic that has developed from childhood.

Some of the various methods of accessing Script we have mentioned earlier on in the Chapter. There are many more techniques available, but Transactional Analysis provides, I believe, a good method of understanding our Script, overcoming compulsions and facilitating the process of personal transformation. This transformation does not happen overnight. Having created a way of being in the world from an early age, people cannot expect the changes to happen with the flick of a switch. However, change *is* possible, and life offers us many opportunities to become the sort of person we were destined to become.

A Final Word

Personality adaptations or types point to the amazing human spirit in each of us. We adapt to the most difficult circumstances in creative and ingenious ways. Events happen, and we are impacted often to the detriment of our potential for growth. But we manage.

I do not want to give the impression that personality adaptations are in the same league as personality disorders. Far from it. What they represent are the best attempts we made to survive well in this world and be

Transformation

acceptable to the people who were our first carers and to the society in which we grew up. Personality adaptations are the ways we have learnt to be in this world, which have helped us go through life, managing our various behaviours and interacting with the behaviours of others.

Transformation, however, refuses to accept that survival is what we are about. Nor is performing in certain ways to gain acceptance our best way forward.

We are not meant to live half-lives, where our full potential is trapped by the memories of our past. We are all called to the fullness of life, and as we discover the ways we adapted to life instead of being self-aware, spontaneous and intimate, we will find the key to our transformation. I think it was Cardinal Newman who said something like, 'to live is to change, and to have lived fully is to have changed often!' (Newman, 1909: section 1:7). By committing ourselves to embark on the journey of transformation, and by setting out and taking the first step, we will begin an exciting adventure of hope and possibility that can only lead to personal and societal transformation.

References

Bader, E. & Pearson, P. http://www.couplesinstitute.com

Berne, E. (1961) *Transactional Analysis The Classic Handbook to its Principles.* New York: Grove Press.

Berne, E. (1964) *Games People Play. The Psychology of Human Relationships.* London: Penguin.

Berne, E. (1966) *Principles of Group Treatment.* New York: Grove Press.

Berne, E. (1970,1973) *Sex in Human Loving.* London: Penguin.

Berne, E. (1972) *What do You Say, after You Say Hello.* London: André Deutsch.

Camus, A. (First Published in 1942. This edition: 2005) *The Myth of Sisyphus.* London: Penguin Books.

Caroselli, M. (2000) *Leadership Skills for Managers.* New York: McGraw-Hill.

Clark, B.C. (1991) 'Empathic Transactions In The Deconfusion Of The Child Ego States.' *Transactional Analysis Journal.* 21(4): 312-315.

Clarkson, P. & Gilbert, M. (1988) 'Berne's Original Model of Ego States: Some Theoretical Considerations.' *Transactional Analysis Journal.* 18(1): 20-29.

Covey, S. (1989) *The Seven Habits of Highly Effective People.* New York: Simon & Shuster.

Drye, R.C. (1974) 'Stroking the Rebellious Child. An Aspect of managing Resistance. *Transactional Analysis Journal.* 4(3): 23-26.

English, F. (1972) 'Rackets and Real Feelings. Part II.' *Transactional Analysis Journal.* 2(1): 23-25.

English, F. (1976) 'Racketeering.' *Transactional Analysis Journal.* 6(1): 78-81.

Erskine, R. G. (1996) 'Methods of Integrative Psychotherapy.' *Transactional Analysis Journal.* 26(4): 316-328.

Gibson, D. (2014) *Are We Together? Community Life in Action.* Dublin: Cluain Mhuire Press.

Hay, L. (1984) *You Can Heal Your Life.* United States: Hay House Inc.

Holloway, W.H. (1972) 'The Crazy Child in the Parent.' *Transactional Analysis Journal.* 2 (3): 32-34.

Joines, V. (1986) 'Using redecision therapy with different personality adaptations.' *Transactional Analysis Journal.* 16(3): 152-160.

Joines, V. (2002) Workshop presentation/handout.

Joines, V. (2014) Personal Communication.

Joines, V. & Stewart, I. (2002) *Personality Adaptations.* Melton Mowbray & Chapel Hill: Lifespace Publishing.

Kahler, T. (1975) 'Drivers: The Key to the Process of Scripts.' *Transactional Analysis Journal.* 5(3): 280-284.

Kahler, T. (1979) *Process Therapy in Brief. The Clinical Application of Miniscript.* Little Rock: Human Development Publications.

Kahler, T. (1978) *Transactional Analysis Revisited.* Little Rock: Human Development Publications.

Kahler, T. (2008) *The Process Therapy Model.* Little Rock: Taibi Kahler Associates.

Korthuis, J. (2006) *Desirable Power. Take Control of Your Life, Health and Relationships.* Florida: BCE Institute.

Myers, L.B. & Myers, P.B. (1980) *Gifts Differing. Understanding Personality Type.* California: Mountain View

Newman, J.H. (1909) *An Essay on the Development of Christian Doctrine.* London: Longmans, Green & Co.

Riso, D.R. & Hudson, R. (1999) *The Wisdom of the Enneagram. The Complete Guide to Psychological and Spiritual Growth for the Nine Personality Types.* New York: Bantam Books.

Schiff, J.L. in collaboration with Schiff, A.W.; Mellor, K.; Schiff, E.; Schiff ,S.; Richman, D.; Fishman, J.; Wolz, L.; Fishman,C. & Momb,D. (1975) *Cathexis Reader. Transactional Analysis Treatment of Psychoses.* New York, Evanston, San Francisco, and London: Harper & Row.

Schore, A.N. (2003) *Affect Regulation and the Repair of the Self.* London: Norton.

Schore, A.N. (2012) *The Science of the Art of Psychotherapy.* London: Norton.

Spitz, R. (1945) 'Hospitalism, Genesis of Psychiatric Conditions in Early Childhood.' *Psychoanalytic Study of the Child.* 1: 53-74.

Strachan, D. (2007) *Making Questions Work: A Guide to What and How to Ask for Facilitators, Consultants, Managers, Coaches, and Educators.* San Francisco: Jossey-Bass.

Ware, P. (1983) 'Personality Adaptations (Doors to Therapy)' *Transactional Analysis Journal,* 13(1): 11-19.

SUGGESTED READING FOR A STUDY OF TRANSACTIONAL ANALYSIS

BASIC TEXTS:

James, M. & Jongeward, D. (1996) *Born to Win: Transactional Analysis with Gestalt Experiments.* Cambridge: Perseus Books. Interesting and Enjoyable.

Sills, C. & Lapworth, P. (2011) *An Introduction to Transactional Analysis: Helping People Change.* London: Sage. A short introduction to TA.

Steiner, C. (1974) *Scripts People Live: Transactional Analysis of Life Scripts.* New York: Grove Press. Written by one of the early TA colleagues of Eric Berne. Worth reading.

Stewart, I., & Joines, V. (1987; 2nd Edition, 2012) *TA Today: A New Introduction to Transactional Analysis.* Nottingham: Lifespace. The best textbook for introducing people to TA and suitable for students and lay people alike.

Stewart, I. (1996) *Developing Transactional Analysis Counselling.* London: Sage. A valuable resource for therapists who have a good understanding of TA.

Tilney, T. (1998) *Dictionary of Transactional Analysis.* London: Wiley-Blackwell. A great book to revise TA theory once the basics have been covered.

Tudor, K. (Ed.) (2002) *Transactional Analysis Approaches to Brief Therapy or What do you say between saying hello and goodbye?* London: Sage. Useful essays of various aspects of TA for the student of TA.

Widdowson, M. (2010) *Transactional Analysis: 100 Key Points & Techniques.* London & New York: Routledge. An excellent book for people familiar with TA theory.

Author Index

Allen & Fonagy: 144

Bader & Pearson: 137,139-140
Berne: 6,22-25,27,82,91,
105-106,110,145-146,
154-155, 160-161

Camus: 111
Caroselli: 2
Clark: 144
Clarkson & Gilbert: 92
Covey: 141

Drye: 28

English: 47
Erskine: 142,144-146

Gibson: 140
Goulding & Goulding: 160-161

Hay: 164
Holloway: 40

Joines: 8,10,121,156,165
Joines & Stewart: 5,41,
42,49,60,101,106,114-
115,121

Kahler: 5-6,10,32,105,
107,112-113,132,137,148
Korthuis: 159-160

Myers Briggs: 3,157

Newman: 168

Riso & Hudson: 4, 157-158

Schiff: 99,143
Schore: 9
Spitz: 12
Strachan: 143

Ware: 4-6,12,15

Subject Index
(numbers in bold indicate chapter)

Affirmations 164-166
Allowers 148-154

Brilliant Sceptic **6**,
10-11,41-42,
54-63,80,113-115,124,
126-127,130,134,136,142,
162,165

Channels of Communication **14**
    Directive 84,132-136
    Requestive 134,136
    Nurturative 134-136
    Emotive 135-136
Charming Manipulator **7**,
11-12,41,66-74,102,106-108,
114-120,127-129,133-135,
154,158,163,165-166
Contamination 25-28,33,40-41,
48-49,59-60,70-71,82,91-92,
101,120
Creative Daydreamer **5**,
10,41-51,59,80,95-96,100-101,
107-108,117,121,127,130,137,
150,155,165
Cycle of Inquiry 146-147
    Be Calm 140-141,146-147
    Be Curious 140,142-143,
    146-147
    Be Empathic 140,146-147
    Be an Echo 140,145,146

Drivers 32-40,47,57-58,69,
80,90,100, 104-106,
148-149,154

Be Perfect 32-33,40,58-59,
80-81,106,109, 113,148,
Be Strong 32,34-35,47,58,
61, 69-70,80-81,100-101,
106-108, 113,118,148,151
Try Hard 32,35-36,100,106,
108-109,111,113,148,152
Please Others 32,37-38,
69-70,106,110,128,148,
153
Hurry Up 32,38-39,
90-91,101,148,153-154

Ego State Model 24,27
Enneagram 3,157-158
Enthusiastic over-reactor **9**,
10,41-42,87-95,113-116,
122-125,127-128,135-136,
141,163,166
Exclusions 60,71,120

Functional Ego State Model
27-28

Inquirer 137,139-140,144-145,
147

Myers-Briggs 3,157

Open, Target & Trapdoors
15-20,

Performing Adaptations
12-15,41,105,121-122,130,137,
156-157
Permissions **13**

Playful Resisters **10**, 10,13,41-42,96-104, 106,109,113-119,121, 126-127,129-130,133-134, 136,141,156
Process Scripts **11**
    Until 106,109
    After 106,109-110,113
    Almost I & II 106,111-113, 119
    Never 106-108,119,113
    Always 108-109,120
Progressive Mental Alignment (PMA) 159-160

Redecision Therapy 161
Responsible Workaholic **8**, 10-11,43,76-85,106,109, 114-119,123,125,128,134, 152,163, 165-166

Script 22,105-112,119,161, 166-167
Substitute Feelings 46-47,58, 118
Surviving Adaptations 12,13-15,20,41,51,80,105, 121-123,125-128,130,156-157,

Transactional Analysis 6,21-23, 161,167

Printed in Great Britain
by Amazon